THE IRON AGE IN NORTHERN BRITAIN

The Iron Age
in Northern Britain

EDITED BY A.L.F. RIVET

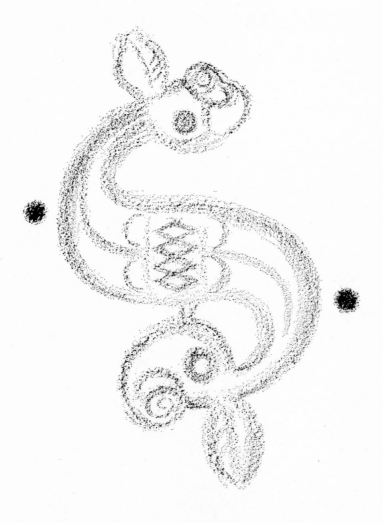

EDINBURGH
at the University Press

© 1966
EDINBURGH UNIVERSITY PRESS
22 George Square, Edinburgh 8
North America
Aldine Publishing Company
320 West Adams Street, Chicago 5
Australia and New Zealand
Hodder & Stoughton Ltd
Africa, Oxford University Press
India, P. C. Manaktala & Sons
Far East, M. Graham Brash & Son

Reprinted 1967, 1968

85224 041 4

Printed in Great Britain
by Robert Cunningham and Sons Ltd., Alva

FOREWORD

The several chapters of this book represent revised versions of the papers delivered by their authors to the Conference on Problems of the Iron Age in Northern Britain held in Edinburgh in October 1961. The Conference was organised, by the Iron Age and Roman Research Committee of the Council for British Archaeology, as a complement to that held in London three years previously on Problems of the Iron Age in Southern Britain, and on that account the southern boundary of the area to be considered was somewhat loosely defined. For the purpose of publication, however, the Committee felt that greater coherence would be obtained by restricting the scope of the volume to Northern Britain proper, that is, to the area lying north of the Tyne–Solway line. A summary of the papers now omitted will be found in *Antiquity*, Volume XXXVI, 1962, pages 24-31.

Even within its more limited field this volume does not pretend to cover the Iron Age of Northern Britain completely. A brief conspectus both of the history of its study and of the state of knowledge regarding it is indeed provided by Professor Piggott's opening chapter, but thereafter the authors deal separately with selected subjects, and some aspects of the matter are inevitably neglected. Secondly, as commonly occurs in cooperative works of this nature, there have been delays both in completion and in publication, and in general the chapters represent the authors' thoughts at times varying from 1961 to 1964, when the volume was completed. Nevertheless it is hoped that by bringing together these authoritative surveys and statements the book may serve both as a useful work of reference and as a stimulus to further research.

A.L.F.R.
Keele, 1966

ACKNOWLEDGMENTS

Thanks are due to the following for permission to make use of copyright and unpublished material: The Ministry of Public Building and Works, The Royal Commission on the Ancient and Historical Monuments of Scotland, The Society of Antiquaries of Newcastle upon Tyne and The Society of Antiquaries of Scotland; and to the British Museum and the National Museum of Antiquities of Scotland for supplying photographs.

The map on page 46 was drawn by Mrs Steel, those on pages 90 and 99 by Mr G. Jobey, and the remainder, including the folding map, by Mr I. G. Scott.

CONTENTS

ABBREVIATIONS
used in the Bibliography and Notes

Ant.	Antiquity
Ant.J	Antiquaries Journal
Arch.	Archaeologia
Arch.Ael.	Archaeologia Aeliana
Arch.Camb.	Archaeologia Cambrensis
Arch.J	Archaeological Journal
Arch.Scot.	Archaeologia Scotica
C.B.A.	Council for British Archaeology
H Berwick NC	History of the Berwickshire Naturalists' Club
J Cork HAS	Journal of the Cork Historical and Archaeological Society
J Galway AHS	Journal of the Galway Archaeological and Historical Society
JRSAI	Journal of the Royal Society of Antiquaries of Ireland
Nat.Mus.Ants.	National Museum of Antiquities of Scotland
P Falkirk ANHS	Proceedings of the Falkirk Archaeological and Natural History Society
PPS	Proceedings of the Prehistoric Society
PRIA	Proceedings of the Royal Irish Academy
PSAN	Proceedings of the Society of Antiquaries of Newcastle upon Tyne
PSAS	Proceedings of the Society of Antiquaries of Scotland
R.C.A.H.M.(S)	Royal Commission on Ancient and Historical Monuments of Scotland
R.C.H.M.(E)	Royal Commission on Historical Monuments (England)
Rev.Celt	Revue Celtique
T Bute NHS	Transactions of the Buteshire Natural History Society
TC & WAAS	Transactions of the Cumberland and Westmorland Antiquarian and Archaeological Society
TD & GNHAS	Transactions of the Dumfriesshire and Galloway Natural History and Antiquarian Society
T Glasgow AS	Transactions of the Glasgow Archaeological Society
TRIA	Transactions of the Royal Irish Academy
UJA	Ulster Journal of Archaeology
Yorks AJ	Yorkshire Archaeological Journal

Chapter One

A SCHEME FOR
THE SCOTTISH IRON AGE

STUART PIGGOTT

The recognition of the Scottish Iron Age has itself a respectable antiquity; Allan Ramsay includes brochs under the style of 'Pictish Towers'
as an essentially Scottish type of monument in his Ode to the Society of
Antiquaries of London of 1726;[1] John Williams published his remarkable
essay on vitrified forts in 1777;[2] and in the first volume of *Archaeologia
Scotica* (1792) there are communications not only on brochs and duns in
Lewis, but on the earthworks of Burnswark, identifying the hill-fort as
'the refuge of the natives in the time of the Romans'.[3] Hill-fort studies
were continued in the nineteenth century, culminating in Christison's
general survey published in 1898,[4] while Munro's research on crannogs
was summarised in his book of 1882.[5] In the following year, the publication of Anderson's third series of Rhind Lectures presented a conspectus not only of several classes of field monument, but of other elements
of Iron Age material culture, notably the metal-work.[6]

In the present century we move into a more recognisably modern
world with the appearance of James Curle's Newstead volume of 1911,[7]
which, although concerned with a Roman fort, illuminated in no small
degree the problems of the native cultures of southern Scotland, as did
his subsequent studies, and those of his brother, over the whole country.
From 1909 onwards the Royal Commission on Ancient and Historical
Monuments for Scotland began publishing the results of its field-work,
which was to have an increasing bearing on Scottish Iron-Age studies as
time went on.

The first treatment of the subject that one can regard as modern in
approach was, as in almost all fields of Scottish prehistory, that of Childe

in 1935.[8] Much material had been amassed since the end of the nineteenth century, but Scottish archaeology, after the brilliant lead given by
such as Anderson, Munro, Abercromby, and James Curle, had moved
into a distressing period of isolation. Excavation and field techniques
were at a shockingly low level, and out of touch with contemporary developments south of the Border, while comparative studies were similarly
stultified and parochial. This led to an unfortunate climate of thought
prevailing, in which Scottish prehistory was regarded as something *sui
generis*; inaccessible and strange, couched in a secret language of broch
and wag, weem and dun, and not to be regarded as a part of the wider
British scene. Too often English distribution maps were made which
faded out around the line of Hadrian's Wall, and the uncritical accept-
ance as an immutable law of Fox's generalised thesis that British prehistory in part reflected the geographers' concept of a Highland and a
Lowland Zone, led inevitably to the relegation of Scotland as a peripheral area, so retarded culturally and chronologically as to render it an
Ultima Thule without significance to the main stream of British or
European prehistory.

The Scottish Iron Age suffered perhaps a greater degree of neglect
than the phases preceding it on account of a cardinal distinction between
the evidence for British prehistory in the first millennium B.C. in the
south and in the north. In the second millennium, the quantities of
Beakers, Food Vessels and Cinerary Urns in North Britain, as in the
South, made it almost impossible for any but the most chauvinistic to
regard the two as separate and isolated provinces. In the south, the abun-
dance of pottery as archaeological evidence continues uninterruptedly up
to the Roman Conquest, and the basic structure of the southern English
Iron Age has been devised within a ceramic framework. But in northern
England, and in much of Scotland, pottery later than the Bronze Age is
either virtually non-existent, or, when present (as for instance in the
Broch and Wheel-House Cultures) is normally of insular types with at
best tenuous relationships to any of the main British series.

This distinction in the type of archaeological evidence between Scotland and southern England is crucial: it is axiomatic that the type of evidence conditions the type of prehistory that can be based upon it. For
the more southerly regions we have a range of evidence which includes
pottery, metal-work, settlements and hill-forts, but in the north we have
to place our reliance to a far greater extent on the field monuments of
earthwork or stone, unsupported by collateral ceramic evidence.

It follows from this that one of the most significant contributions to
our knowledge of the Scottish Iron Age, especially for the Lowlands, has
been that of the Royal Commission on Ancient Monuments over the past

fifteen years. The new approach to field monuments involving air photo-
graphy on the one hand, and on the other the structural analysis of complex monuments on the ground, disentangling their chronological components by a process analogous to the investigation of the architectural
phases of the ancient building, has revolutionised our knowledge and
understanding of that area of Scotland where contacts with the rest of
Britain are most likely to exist. And on the basis of this field-work, the
prosecution of selective excavations on significant sites has taken the
matter a stage further.

With this as an introduction, we can now turn to our main task—to
attempt a classification of the Scottish Iron Age in cultural and chronological terms comparable with those used by Hawkes for England.[9] His
scheme involved a structure based on three main factors: geography,
chronology, and culture. For the first, he divided England and Wales
into five major natural provinces, containing thirty subordinate regions.
In 1956 I put forward a tentative scheme for recognising four major areas
in the Scottish Iron Age, which we can, it seems, retain as provinces;
these are Atlantic, Solway-Clyde, Tyne-Forth and North-Eastern.[10] Ap-
plying his detailed knowledge of the field monuments in their geographical setting, Feachem has divided these four provinces into twenty-two
regions, numbered consecutively from 31 to 52, following on Hawkes's
thirty regions for England and Wales, and this scheme for the Scottish
provinces and regions is set out on a map (fig. 1), and demonstrated in
detail by Feachem in Chapter 4.

For chronology, Hawkes used a system of periods and subordinate
phases, with absolute dates derived from Continental (and ultimately
historical Mediterranean) evidence. These I follow in their major divisions, the Scottish evidence not being adequate at present for the detec-
tion of phases. Iron 1, c. 550-350 B.C., and Iron 2, c. 350-150 B.C., are
unaltered, but to suit the northern material I end Iron 3 (beginning
c. 150 B.C.) at c. 80 A.D., and add an Iron 4, from this date to an uncertain lower limit in the third century A.D. or later, to denote native cultures
contemporary with or surviving later than the Roman Occupation of
Scotland.

The definition of cultures is naturally our most difficult task, but we
may begin by considering the background to any Iron-Age scheme, that
of the Bronze Age. The recent recognition that the Cordoned and En-
crusted Cinerary Urns do not, in any meaningful terms, fall into a Late
Bronze Age, but belong to its early and middle phase within the second
millennium B.C., has virtually bereft Scotland of burials, and left her
very little pottery, appropriate to the periods immediately before and at
the time of the first establishment of iron-using communities. Coles's

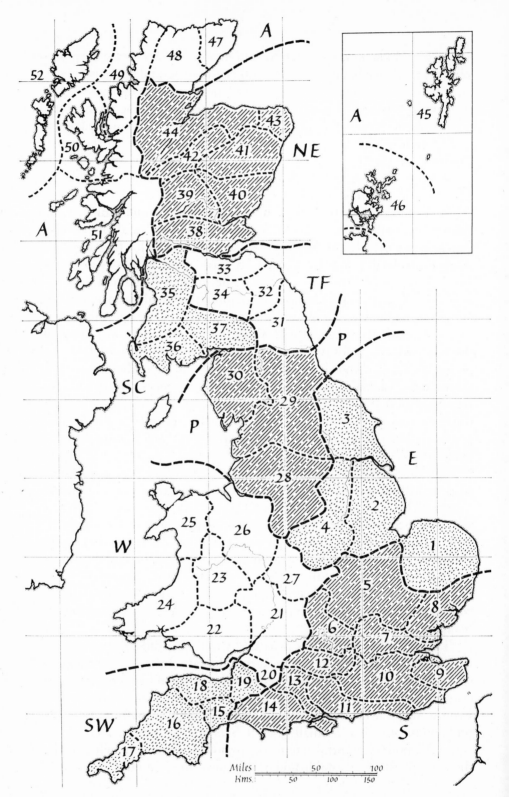

Fig. 1. British Iron-Age Provinces and Regions; for Key see opposite page.

Provinces and Regions of the British Iron Age

Eastern Province (E)
  1. Norfolk and borders; 2. Kesteven/Lindsey; 3. Eastern Yorkshire; 4. Trent basin.

Southern Province (S)
  5. Nene/Cambridge; 6. Upper Thames; 7. Thames/Lea; 8. Chelmer/Ipswich;
  9. East Kent/Medway; 10. Thames/Wealden; 11. South Downs, with Wight;
  12. North Wessex; 13. Mid-Wessex; 14. South Wessex.

South-Western Province (SW)
  15. East Devon; 16. Dartmoor/Cornwall; 17. West Cornwall; 18. Exmoor/Quan-
  tock; 19. Mid-Somerset.

Western Province (W)
  20. East Somerset; 21. Wye/Cotswold; 22. South Wales; 23. Mid-Wales; 24. West
  Wales; 25. North Wales; 26. Northern Marches; 27. West Midland.

Pennine Province (P)
  28. South Pennine; 29. North Pennine; 30. Cumbria.

Tyne-Forth Province (TF)
  31. Northumberland; 32. Lower Tweeddale; 33. Lothian; 34. Upper Tweeddale/
  Upper Clydesdale.

Solway-Clyde Province (SC)
  35. Strathclyde; 36. Galloway; 37. Dumfries.

North-Eastern Province (NE)
  38. Strathearn; 39. Strathtay; 40. Strathmore; 41. Strathdon/Strathdee;
  42. Strathspey; 43. Buchan; 44. Cromarty/Moray.

Atlantic Province (A)
  45. Shetland; 46. Orkney; 47. Caithness; 48. Strathnaver; 49. Cape Wrath/Wester
  Ross; 50. Skye/Western Inverness-shire; 51. Argyll/Bute; 52. Outer Hebrides.

Eastern, Southern, South-Western, Western and Pennine Provinces and Regions 1-30
after C. F. C. Hawkes, *The ABC of the British Iron Age* (1959).

recent work[11] has defined, however, a Covesea phase dating from the mid-eighth, and in the main of the seventh century B.C.; this period is named from the Covesea type of what has previously been vaguely defined as 'Flat Rimmed Ware'. This phase is partly contemporary in Scotland with a Duddingston phase beginning in the mid-eighth century, and reflects influences chiefly from the Hallstatt C phase of the Continent, with in east Scotland evidence of contacts with North Germany, and in the west, trade contributions from the workshops making beaten bronze cauldrons and buckets. In the Adabrock and Tarves phases, the former from before 600 B.C., the Hallstatt C tradition still continues although the central Hallstatt area of the Continent was now developing the D phase from *c*. 600; the Tarves phase is linked to eastern England and, as earlier, with North Europe. Fragments of a cross-handle-holder bowl from Adabrock in Lewis are of Central European Hallstatt C type, as are the mountings probably of a miniature cult-wagon from Horsehope in Peebleshire. Native bronze swords of late Ewart Park type were in use and, as moulds demonstrate, were being locally made at Traprain in East Lothian and Jarlshof in Shetland. In the Tarves phase, from the sixth century B.C., a specifically Scottish type of bronze 'sunflower' pin with crooked stem can be recognised, with North German prototypes and associated with late Ewart swords at the type-site of Tarves in Aberdeenshire;[12] such pins are comparable with one (of bronze and iron) from the Iron Eastern First A site at Peterborough, Northants.[13] Within this period would also come the first of the two 'Late Bronze Age' settlements at Jarlshof in Shetland (with its sword-moulds); the second, as we shall see, is better classified as Iron Atlantic First A. The Adabrock-Tarves phase of our Scottish Late Bronze Age will then in part be contemporary with such Eastern First A sites as Peterborough (already quoted), Scarborough (N.R. Yorks), or Staple Howe in the East Riding: here a radiocarbon date of 450 ± 150 B.C. (BM-63) broadly confirms the evidence of the presumably late seventh-century Hallstatt C razors from the site.[14] We must remember these North German contacts with Scotland, at least up to the beginning of the fifth century B.C., for they need not have been restricted to those phases nominally confined to the final Bronze Age of the north.

As in the whole of the British Isles, a difficulty in distinguishing immigrant and intrusive Iron-Age cultures in any region, in the absence of characteristic pottery or metal-work, is caused by the retention in all our insular cultures of the circular house-plan whose antecedents go back at least to the beginning of the second millennium B.C. or even beyond. Despite the fact that the Continental ancestors of all our immigrant cultural groups of the first millennium B.C., whether technologically bronze- or iron-working, built variants of rectangular houses, even our earliest Iron-Age sites, such as West Harling or Staple Howe, have circular house-plans. In Scotland, where structures have so largely to be used as cultural determinants in default of pottery, it is scarcely possible to assign sites with timber-framed circular houses and palisaded enclosures to a precise cultural setting if other evidence is not forthcoming, but the recent excavation at Green Knowe in Peeblesshire of a circular, double-walled, timber-framed house in a settlement of 'unenclosed platform' type, along with a pot of the Flat Rimmed class,[15] shows that at least some such sites may fall within Coles's final phases of the Scottish Late Bronze Age.

At Jarlshof in Shetland, the stone-built house-type in both the Late Bronze Age phase, and that assignable to Atlantic First A of the Iron Age, is that derived from the early to middle second millennium B.C. forms such as Gruting or Stanydale. But to return to the lowland timber houses and their enclosures; some of these may in fact be of the Late Bronze Age, and others constitute an early element in Tyne-Forth First A, described below.

In the North-East Region we are faced with an analogous problem presented by the hill-forts with timber-laced or vitrified walls. Some of these have produced objects which enable us to assign them to a North-Eastern Second A, which we must again discuss at a later stage; but unexcavated examples, or those where digging has produced no dating evidence, need not be so late as this. Remembering the North German contacts with Scotland in the Covesea and Tarves phases, we may also note that timber-laced ramparts and walls on the Continent go back at least to Hallstatt B3 (current dating eighth century B.C.), as at the Wittnauer Horn in Switzerland;[16] and in North Germany Late Urnfield forts (but probably not later than c. 600 B.C.), such as the Kratzeburg or the Schlossberg near Witzen, as well as others, have timber-laced ramparts.[17] On the other hand, as Mrs Cotton has pointed out, the technique of timber-lacing in the Scottish forts, with its absence of vertical timbers set in post-holes in the natural soil, differentiates them from her pre-Caesarian Preist (or Altkönig-Preist) type, and allies them in some measure with her 'devolved Avaricum' group, which would be not much earlier than the *murus gallicus* as described by Caesar at Avaricum itself and other Gaulish sites—certainly not earlier than c. 100 B.C.[18] The North German Late Urnfield forts just mentioned have in fact upright timbers to the front and rear of the rampart, and presumably represent forms ancestral to Preist (itself La Tène II, second century B.C.); but at the Wittnauer Horn, both in the Hallstatt B3 and the Hallstatt C/D phases of construction, there were no vertical posts, only horizontal members.

It may be, then, that two variant styles of timber-lacing were already current in Late Urnfield times: Mrs Cotton has noted how some vitrified forts in North-East France had only transverse timbering.[19]

Turning now to the sites and objects which can be brought into the Iron-Age scheme, we may begin with a First A, recognisable in the Tyne-Forth and the Atlantic Provinces. *Tyne-Forth First A* will be represented by some at least of the palisaded enclosures with timber-framed houses even if others may belong to a hypothetical earlier phase within the Late Bronze Age; so, too, the palisaded enclosures demonstrated by excavation to be earlier than stone-wall or rampart defences on hill-fort sites—Hownam I, the first phase of the Hownam Rings fort, falls here.[20] Absolute dating is unobtainable directly, but stratigraphy shows that it should come before Tyne-Forth Second A, itself in the second century B.C. as we shall see below, and it is suggested that we may place our Tyne-Forth First A late in Period 1 and early in Period 2, *c.* 400–250 B.C.

Atlantic First A is represented by 'Late Bronze-Age Village II' at Jarlshof.[21] Mr Stevenson has pointed out to me that the evidence for only a short hiatus between this and 'Village I' (a piece of a sword-mould of the Late Bronze Age in House IVb of 'Village II') is very uncertain: the fragment may easily be derived, as indeed the original excavator himself thought. At all events, the pottery which we fortunately have from 'Village II' is itself comparable with that from other peripheral First A sites in England and Wales, such as Kestor, Bodrifty, and Castell Odo, the relevant phase of the last site being dated by its excavator to *c.* 325 B.C.[22] Approximate contemporaneity between the First A cultures of the Tyne-Forth and the Atlantic Provinces may then be reasonably accepted. The Late Bronze-Age houses at Jarlshof, as we have seen, are typological descendants of those of the Gruting-Stanydale class,[23] and the main house of the Iron First A settlement, no. IVb, is a further modification and an insular development of this plan. The structure is now roughly circular instead of oval, with a series of bays between projecting piers around a hearth—a layout which in its turn is antecedent to the later round-house and wheel-house series on the site, characteristic of Atlantic Second B and scattered elsewhere in Scotland.

The stratigraphy in the Tyne-Forth Province just mentioned shows us that apart from the palisaded enclosures they sometimes overlay, the earliest defensive structures are hill-forts consisting of a sheer-faced wall, or with stone facing and a rubble or earthen filling. These on occasion have horizontal timbering related to the fully timber-laced walls of the forts in the North-East Province. With these Tyne-Forth wall-forts we can associate ring-headed pins, spiral finger-rings, La Tène IC brooches, and penannular brooches of Elizabeth Fowler's Aa class.[24] It is probable

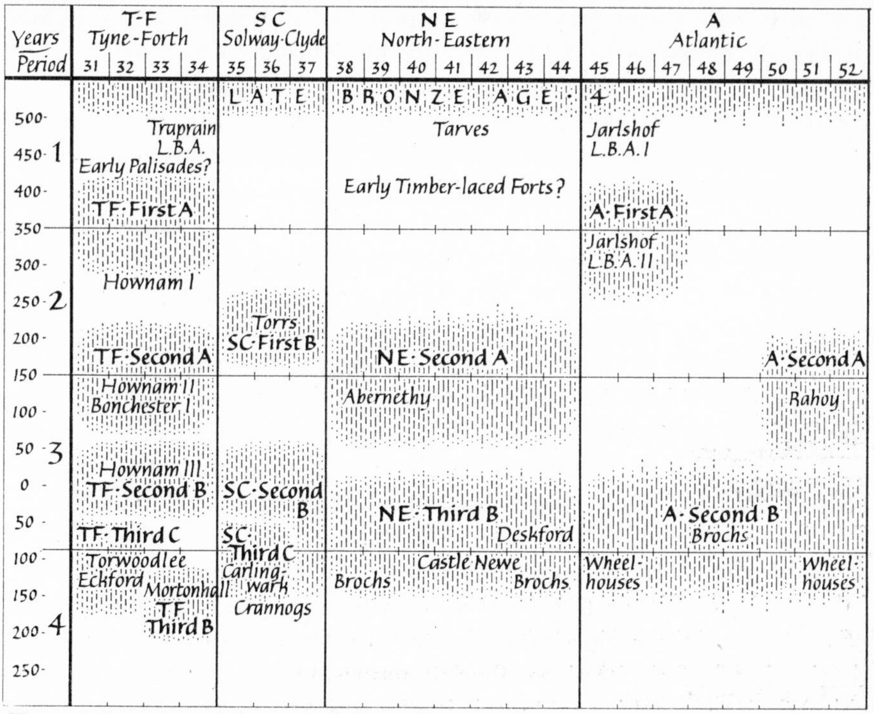

Years / Period	T-F Tyne-Forth 31 32 33 34	S C Solway-Clyde 35 36 37	N E North-Eastern 38 39 40 41 42 43 44	A Atlantic 45 46 47 48 49 50 51 52
		LATE	BRONZE AGE 4	
500 — 1 450 — 400 —	Traprain L.B.A. Early Palisades? TF-First A		Tarves Early Timber-laced Forts?	Jarlshof L.B.A. I A-First A
350 — 300 — 250 — 2 200 — 150 —	Hownam I TF-Second A	Torrs SC-First B	NE-Second A	Jarlshof L.B.A. II A-Second A
100 — 50 — 3 0 — 50 —	Hownam II Bonchester I Hownam III TF-Second B TF-Third C	SC-Second B SC-Third C	Abernethy NE-Third B Deskford	Rahoy A-Second B Brochs
100 — 150 — 200 — 4 250 —	Torwoodlee Eckford Mortonhall TF Third B	Carlingwark Crannogs	Castle Newe Brochs Brochs	Wheel-houses Wheel-houses

Fig. 2. *Scheme for the North British Iron Age.*

that saddle, rather than rotary, querns are also characteristic. These are mainly types referable to Second A cultures in southern England, and they may therefore be taken as representing a *Tyne-Forth Second A*; the La Tène brooches, which would in the Southern and South-Western Provinces of England be appropriate to First or Second B, must here be either trade objects acquired by members of a basically A culture, or, where not in any strict archaeological association, belong to the Second B cultures later to be discussed. As to chronology, we need no longer feel a necessity to date the Scottish material in terms of the latest possible appearance of the respective types in the south, and, furthermore, the recent reassessment of southern English absolute chronology for this period raises the dates of such contexts as Maiden Castle Phase III, previously used to support a low chronology.[25] We may perfectly well take the beginnings of Tyne-Forth Second A to the earlier second century B.C., late in Period 2; then or soon after we should have the early wall-forts such as Hownam II (overlying the palisades of Hownam I), and Bonchester I, with their counterparts, doubtless continuing in construction to the end of the century.

The La Tène Ic and Aa penannular brooches (as well as occasional timbering in the walls of Tyne-Forth forts, such as is found by the gateway of Castle Law, Glencorse)[26] connect that province with other sites previously classified by Childe within his Abernethy Culture,[27] where we can recognise a *North-Eastern Second A*, including certain timber-laced wall forts. We have seen that forts of this construction could in fact occur at an early date in Scotland owing to her North German contacts in the Late Bronze Age, unshared by England at the time; but in the main we have no evidence against making our North-Eastern Second A contemporaneous with its Tyne-Forth counterpart. Even so, if we are to place its beginnings in the second century B.C., we cannot consider the timber-laced forts to be derived from the Avaricum type of Caesarian date, but must seek another origin, perhaps, ultimately as suggested above, in Late Urnfield traditions which survive to form counterparts to the Preist type of construction in La Tène times. At all events, the site of Rahoy,[28] with a La Tène Ic brooch and wall-timbering, would represent an *Atlantic Second A* of comparable date to that of the North-Eastern Province.

With the B group of cultures we have at the outset the difficulties inherent in fine decorated metal-work, which may so easily be an object of trade or of the reciprocal exchange of gifts, and so find an eventual destination far from its place of manufacture. The Torrs (Kirkcudbrightshire) find[29] poses this problem: is it a local product of the Solway-Clyde Province or an import, perhaps from the Eastern Province of England? A Scottish origin is supported by the fact that motifs characteristic of the Torrs style are utilised on later, and unquestionably Scottish, pieces such as the Stichill collar and the Plunton Castle armlet;[30] we may therefore tentatively use Torrs to indicate the existence of a *Solway-Clyde First B*, for which the stylistic features of the metal-work, not far removed from the Continental Waldalgesheim style, would demand a date around 200 B.C.

The Second B cultures as defined by Hawkes for England constitute the counterparts of the European La Tène II culture, and their components include not only characteristic pottery and metal-work, but bivallate or multivallate hill-forts. In southern Scotland we can therefore group multiple wall or multiple rampart forts (such as the defences of Hownam III) with metal-work represented by scabbard-chapes of my Group III from Glencotho (Peeblesshire) and Hounslow (Berwickshire),[31] to form a *Tyne-Forth Second B*. Into this, too, would come the few bone weaving-combs and 'toggles' that have survived in the acid soils of the province, a bronze terret and bridle-bits from Newstead,[32] and also the gold torc-terminal from Netherurd ('Cairnmuir') (Peeblesshire), closely paralleled at Snettisham, Eastern Second B of the early first century B.C.[33] Dating is difficult and imprecise but the culture should probably begin about the middle of Period 3, following the Tyne-Forth Second A in the first century B.C., and continuing into the beginning of Period 4, and the first Roman impact.

Weaving-combs and 'toggles' in the Solway-Clyde province (for example, in the Borness Cave and elsewhere)[34] are pointers to a comparable situation there, supported by such metal-work as the bronze and iron bits, that from the Lochlee crannog being of a type closely resembling those of English Eastern Second B at Stanwick, and others (for example, from Middlebie, Birrenswark, and East Kilbride) being later versions comparable with the Newstead bits.[35] The Balmaclellan mirror-handle, with ornament of Eastern Second B affinities, and the other objects in the find with incised mirror-style ornament should again belong here.[36] We may therefore see a *Solway-Clyde Second B*, in which the individual circular farmstead appears as a crannog of the Lochlee-Milton Loch type: origins may lie at the end of Period 3 but the culture continues well into Period 4, as the metal-work and other decorated objects, and associations with Roman material, show.

Weaving-combs, bone bobbins, parallelepiped dice and other objects such as the whale-bone loop-handle from North Uist—an exact skeuomorph of one in bronze from Lochlee[37]—give substance, together with the circular farmstead settlement of wheel-house or broch type, to an important *Atlantic Second B* culture. Here the circular stone-built house in its various forms (wheel-house, round-house, broch) seems to have multiple origins, deriving in part from the second millennium Gruting-Stanydale traditions (seen in a developed transitional form in House ivb in the First A settlement at Jarlshof), and in part from the timber-built single farmsteads ultimately of Little Woodbury type, represented by the crannogs of the Solway-Clyde Second B culture or (as we shall see) by sites such as West Plean or Scotstarvit in North-Eastern Third B. The internal sequence of house types, and of the spread of the culture within the Province, are among the problems to be elucidated: chronologically, a beginning for Atlantic Second B late in Period 3, and an undefined continuance into Period 4, seem as much as we can safely say at present.

For cultures still within the B tradition, but demonstrably or inferentially later, we must use the term Third B. The Mortonhall sword-scabbard of my Group IV, and other metal-work such as the Stanhope (Peeblesshire) find[38] and the Stichill (Roxburghshire) collar, suggest a *Tyne-Forth Third B* to which perhaps the souterrains of that province might also be assigned—at Castle Law, Glencorse, stratigraphically later than the second phase of the fort, presumptively a work of Second B[39]—and the few brochs. Dating here would probably be wholly within Period 4, although a slightly earlier origin is not excluded.

A *North-Eastern Third B* is substantiated by metal-work, brochs, and souterrains, farmsteads such as West Plean or Scotstarvit,[40] and perhaps by the later hill-forts of the Province. The metal-work includes types which I defined as 'Caledonian' in 1948: the bronze carnyx-mouth in the form of a boar's head from Deskford (Banffshire) may be dated stylistically to about the middle of the first century A.D., at the end of Period 3; and the massive armlets of Castle Newe type, which have features of ornament that follow Deskford typologically, are themselves derivatives of ring-ended torcs of the Snettisham type, represented in Scotland by the Netherurd terminal of Tyne-Forth Second B already referred to.[41] With them may be taken the snake-armlets of Culbin type,[42] and later in the culture the Donside terrets, which appear to be derivatives of Roman military forms and probably belong to the second century A.D.[43] The globular bronze cauldron from Kincardine Moss (Perthshire), having affinities with the Spettisbury and Glastonbury bowls and their congeners, and the cauldron from Ballyedmond (Galway), would also take its place here.[44]

The C group of cultures appears to be represented only by the metal-work hoards and bronze cauldrons of Romano-Belgic type as at Cockburnspath (Berwickshire), and (with no cauldron) Eckford (Roxburghshire), which constitute the evidence for a *Tyne-Forth Third C*. The cauldron and hoard from Carlingwark Loch (Kirkcudbrightshire), the cauldron from Elvanfoot (Lanarkshire), and the enamelled terret of Bapchild type from Auchendolly (Kirkcudbrightshire),[45] enable us to hazard a *Solway-Clyde Third C* as well, though the scattered finds of cauldrons of Santon and Battersea types in the Atlantic and North-Eastern Provinces cannot be regarded as other than trade objects, comparable with their counterparts in Ireland. In both provinces the Third C phase can hardly be earlier than the end of Period 3, and must lie mainly in Period 4.

The foregoing outline scheme, presented as a diagram in fig. 2, is obviously subject to amplification and revision in detail; indeed, other contributors to this symposium have indicated minor alternative classifications and adjustments of chronology here and there. I have deliberately restricted my presentation of the scheme to an outline which may serve as a basis for discussion: in its original form it was an opening address to a conference in which, as I said then, we were making a last-minute effort to see the shape of the wood before we plunged into the trees and undergrowth of detail. I retain it in this form, and claim for it nothing more than a suggested scheme within which our material may be classified. Nevertheless, the main framework seems sound to me, and demonstrates the feasibility of extending the conceptual model devised by Hawkes north of the Border: by doing so, it emphasises the essential coherence between the regional Iron-Age cultures of Britain as a whole, and enables us to view the Scottish material in its rightful setting. What we now need is to test and strengthen the structure, especially by excavations which will obtain more stratigraphical sequences of the type available for some of the Tyne-Forth hill-forts, or sites in Shetland within the Atlantic Province. At all events, the Scottish scheme here set out may stand as a beginning, and as at least an attempt at an ordered system.

Postscript

This essay was written in 1962 and represents the state of knowledge and the modes of thought of that date. The important papers of Euan Mac-Kie, 'Brochs and the Hebridean Iron Age', *Antiquity* XXXIX (1965), 266-78, and 'The Origin and Development of the Broch and Wheelhouse Building Cultures of the Scottish Iron Age', *Proc. Prehist. Soc.* XXXI (1965), 93-146, have not therefore been taken into account.

Notes

1. *Poems* (London, 1800), I, 138.
2. J. Williams, *An Account of some Remarkable Ancient Ruins . . .* (Edinburgh, 1777).
3. *Arch. Scot.* I (1792), 282, 124.
4. D. Christison, *Early Fortifications in Scotland* (1898) Rhind Lectures (1894).
5. R. Munro, *Ancient Scottish Lake-Dwellings . . .* (1882).
6. J. Anderson, *Scotland in Pagan Times; The Iron Age* (1883).
7. J. Curle, *A Roman Frontier Post . . .* (1911).
8. V. G. Childe, *Prehistory of Scotland* (1935).
9. C. F. C. Hawkes, 'The ABC of the British Iron Age', *Ant.* XXXIII (1959), 170, and in S. Frere (ed.) *Problems of the Iron Age in Southern Britain*, 1.
10. R.C.A.H.M.(S), *Roxburgh* (1956), I, 15.
11. J. Coles, 'Scottish Late Bronze Age Metalwork . . .', *PSAS* XCIII (1959-60), 16.
12. J. Coles, 'Scottish Swan's-Neck Sunflower Pins', *PSAS* XCII (1958-9), 1.
13. C. F. C. Hawkes, 'The Early Iron Age Settlement at Fengate, Peterborough', *Arch. J.* C (1945), 188; pin on p. 197.
14. T. C. M. Brewster, *The Excavation of Staple Howe*, 1963.
15. R. W. Feachem, *PSAS* XCIV (1960-1), 79-85.
16. G. Bersu, *Das Wittnauer Horn* (1945); pottery compared to Gündlingen type (p. 79) and so Ha B3 (eighth century B.C.) in Müller-Karpe's classification and chronology; *Chronologie der Urnenfelderzeit . . .* (1959).

17. H. Schubart, 'Jungbronzezeitliche Burgwälle in Mecklenburg', *Prähist. Zeitschr.* XXXIX (1961), 143; K. Tackenburg, 'Die Burgen der Lausitzer Kultur', ibid. XXXIV/V (1949-50), Pt. 2, 18; cf. also ibid. I (1909), 209; XVII (1924), 184. There is now a C14 date of 815±100 (Bln-78) for the Kratzeburg.

18. M. A. Cotton, 'British Camps with Timber-Laced Ramparts', *Arch. J* CXI (1955), 26; ead., 'Muri Gallici', in R. E. M. Wheeler and K. Richardson, *Hill-Forts of Northern France* (1957), 159; ead., 'Relationships between Iron Age Earthworks in France and Britain', *Celticum* I (1961), 103.

19. *Celticum* I, 110.

20. C. M. Piggott, 'The Excavations at Hownam Rings . . .', *PSAS* LXXXIII (1948-9), 193.

21. J. R. C. Hamilton, *Excavations at Jarlshof, Shetland* (1956), 32.

22. D. Dudley, 'An Excavation at Bodrifty . . .', *Arch. J* CXIII (1956), 22; A. Fox, 'Excavations at Kestor', *Trans. Devon Assocn.* LXXXVI (1954), 52; L. Alcock, 'Castell Odo . . .', *Arch. Camb.* (1960), 78.

23. C. S. T. Calder, 'Report on the Discovery of several Stone Age House-sites in Shetland', *PSAS* LXXXIX (1955-6), 340.

24. C. M. Piggott, 'The Excavations at Bonchester Hill, 1950', *PSAS* LXXXIV (1949-50), 113, 129; E. Fowler, 'The Origins and Development of the Penannular Brooch in Europe', *PPS* XXVI (1960), 149.

25. S. Frere, 'Some Problems of the later Iron Age', in *Problems of the Iron Age in S. Britain*, 84.

26. S. Piggott, 'Excavations at Castle Law, Glencorse . . .', *PSAS* LXXXVI (1951-2), 191.

27. V. G. Childe, *Prehist. Comms. Brit. Isles* (1947), 213.

28. Id., 'The Vitrified Fort of Rahoy . . .', *PSAS* LXXII (1937-8), 23.

29. R. J. C. Atkinson and S. Piggott, 'The Torrs Chamfrein', *Arch.* XCVI (1955), 197.

30. Ibid., 233.

31. S. Piggott, 'Swords and Scabbards of the British Early Iron Age', *PPS* XVI (1950), 12.

32. J. Curle, *A Roman Frontier Post . . .* (1911), pl. LXXV, 2, 6.

33. R. R. Clarke, 'The Early Iron Age Treasure from Snettisham, Norfolk', *PPS* XX (1954), 64; R. W. Feachem, 'The "Cairnmuir" Hoard from Netherurd, Peeblesshire', *PSAS* XCI (1957-8), 112.

34. A. J. Corrie, 'On a Cave . . . at Borness, Kirkcudbrightshire', *PSAS* X (1872-4), 476.

35. M. MacGregor, 'The Early Iron Age Metalwork Hoard from Stanwick, N.R. Yorks.', *PPS* XXVIII (1962), 23.

36. C. Fox, *Pattern and Purpose* (1958), 99, 116.

37. L. Scott, 'Gallo-British Colonies', *PPS* XIV (1948), 78; G. Clark, 'Whales

as an Economic Factor in Prehistoric Europe', *Ant.* XXI (1947), 84, pl. II, 2; R. Munro, *Anc. Scottish Lake Dwellings* (1882), 132, fig. 147.

38. J. A. Smith, 'Notice of a Massive Bronze "Late Celtic" Armlet . . .', *PSAS* XV (1880-1), 316.

39. V. G. Childe, 'Excavations at Castlelaw Fort, Midlothian', *PSAS* LXVII (1932-3), 362.

40. K. A. Steer, 'An Early Iron Age Homestead at West Plean . . .', *PSAS* LXXXIX (1955-6), 228; G. Bersu, ' "Fort" at Scotstarvit Covert, Fife', *PSAS* LXXXII (1947-8), 241.

41. S. Piggott, 'The *Carnyx* in Early Iron Age Britain', *Ant. J* XXXIX (1959), 19.

42. J. Anderson, *Scotland in Pagan Times; The Iron Age* (1883), 156ff.

43. H. E. Kilbride-Jones, 'An Aberdeenshire Iron Age Miscellany', *PSAS* LXIX (1934-5), 448; for Roman types cf. Hambleden, Bucks. (*Arch.* LXXI (1920-1), 196); Rockanje, Holland (*Bericht R.O.B. Nederland* III (1952), 1); Pannonia (*Serta Hoffileriana* (1940), 315, pl. XXVII, 3).

44. Kincardine Moss (Perthshire and not Stirlingshire), J. Anderson, 'Notice of a Bronze Cauldron . . .', *PSAS* XIX (1884-5), 313; Ballyedmond, E. Rynne, 'A Bronze Cauldron from Ballyedmond, Co. Galway', *J Galway AHS* XXIX (1960), 1.

45. Hoards and cauldrons, S. Piggott, 'Three Metal-work Hoards of the Roman Period . . .', *PSAS* LXXXVII (1952-3), 1; terret, H. E. Maxwell, 'Notice of an Enamelled Bronze Harness Ornament . . .', *PSAS* XX (1885-6), 396.

Chapter Two

METAL-WORK AND SOME
OTHER OBJECTS IN SCOTLAND AND
THEIR CULTURAL AFFINITIES

ROBERT B. K. STEVENSON

Not many significant new objects have come to light since Gordon Childe's *Prehistory*,[1] for early iron-age sites in southern Scotland generally produce few finds and there has been little excavation elsewhere on the mainland. Opinions, however, about the cultural affinities and chronology even of the most familiar objects have kept changing in the course of study and discovery in Britain as a whole. This chapter summarises ideas as they are at present, and attempts to show how far they produce an outline of historical movements in the various centuries covered. The lengthening of early iron-age chronology now generally accepted should result in our separating types previously thought contemporaneous with one another and in recognising significance in minor differences.

Iron Age A: fifth to second century B.C. Late bronze-age metal objects in Scotland have been studied in detail recently by John Coles, and brought down to the fifth century B.C., but no later.[2] Links with the Continent in Hallstatt C and D, which came up the east coast yet by-passed south-east England, are indicated by a series of hoards. Distribution maps of Irish gold lock-rings and of the Continental bronze bracelets current here for several centuries show central and eastern England as an area unaffected or avoided, a pattern that recurs in later centuries. There is also a concentration in north-east Scotland which suggests that the blanks there in some later maps signify real shortages of the objects concerned, although the negative aspects of distribution maps are even harder to

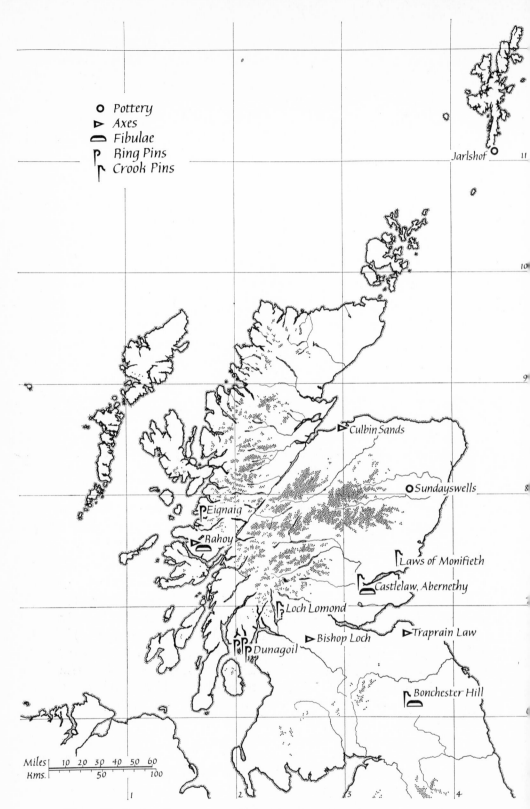

Fig. **1**. *Distribution of pottery, axes, fibulae, ring pins and crook pins.*

inches

Pl. 1 The Torrs 'Chamfrein' as a cap (p. 24), with the horns re-arranged
to accord with the holes being for a pony's ears, not eyes.
(The white infilling of the engraving is a restoration.)
(Photo. National Museum of Antiquities)

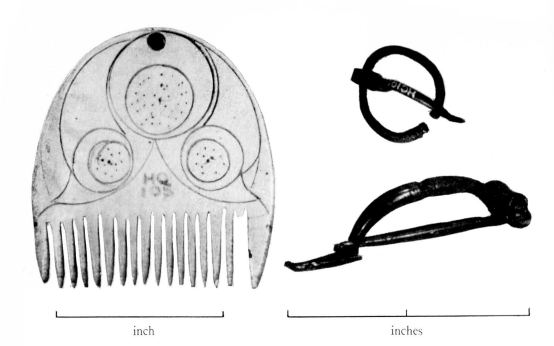

inch

inches

inches

interpret than the positive. Coles has shown further that before the end of our Bronze Age there was developed out of imported ideas, perhaps in central Scotland, a peculiarly Scottish type of *sunflower pin*, with a swan's neck, contemporaneous with the swan's neck pin of the earliest Iron Age in southern England.[3] The pre-existing indigenous population in the background of this and later developments is suggested by the Irish-Scottish *pottery* called *flat-rimmed*, associated with incoming bronzes at Covesea in Morayshire and even Heathery Burn in Yorkshire,[4] a potting tradition that seems to have remained important down to the second century A.D. at Traprain.[5]

In east Yorkshire, however, finer burnished and decorated pottery of West Harling type, Iron First A in Hawkes' terminology, was already associated about 500 B.C. with Hallstatt C razors at Staple Howe,[6] in a palisaded enclosure ancestral to the Cheviot sites described here in Chapter 5. In Scotland a comparable assemblage of earliest iron-age pottery has, remarkably enough, only been found in the far north, at *Jarlshof* in Shetland, with a few sherds in Orkney; it still needs a detailed assessment by someone familiar with the English wares.[7] Unfortunately the significance of this find was obscured in the final excavation report by the name Late Bronze-Age Village II.[8] There was in fact a complete break in continuity after 'Village I', and a new culture appeared—new implements, ornaments and structures, as well as pottery. Yet no long interval need be supposed between the two occupations, for the mould for a sunflower pin (probably Irish) from the late bronze-age workshop and the overlying shouldered pottery could belong to the same century. Moreover, there seems to have been an iron-age infiltration before full-scale invasion, because most, if not all, of the pottery recorded as coming from 'Village I', which had stone implements and house-plans of age-old Shetland tradition, is quite foreign to any part of the flat-rimmed series. The applied fillets and grooves outlining the lip are difficult to place: superficial resemblances to grooved and beaded rims at All Cannings Cross would point to a much later phase of that Wiltshire site. One sherd with chevron decoration in a different style was noted by Childe as thoroughly Hallstatt in effect, and iron slag from a 'Village I' level may also be significant.[9]

There are only slight indications of the other First A groups which must have been absorbed at least in eastern Scotland. One is a bowl,

---

Pl. 2a (above) La Tène Ic fibula from Castlelaw, Abernethy, Perthshire (p. 20);
penannular brooch and bone comb from Langbank Crannog, Renfrewshire (p. 25).
b (below) Four objects from the Lamberton Moor, Berwickshire, hoard, dragonesque
(p. 30) and trumpet brooches, beaded bowl and beaded torc (pp. 26, 31).
(Photos. National Museum of Antiquities)

apparently from a short cist, found at Sundayswells in Aberdeenshire.[10] Another is the frequently discussed *socketed iron axe* from Traprain Law; the excavator recorded it as coming from the habitation site along with bronze axes and other contemporary objects, including a sherd of finger-tipped pottery, and ascribed it to a bronze-iron overlap period. Alternatively the axe has been used as evidence that the Bronze Age in Scotland was prolonged to a very late date.[11] Since, out of the dozen iron axes listed in 1928 (five from the Thames and two more in southern England), this is the one nearest in shape to a bronze axe,[12] the association and approximately fifth-century date ought now to be accepted. It follows that the western slope of Traprain lay unoccupied for a long period before the Roman Iron Age.

A socketed iron axe of the more developed variety, with one straight side, and near it a modified *La Tène Ic* type bronze fibular *brooch*, were found at Rahoy in Morvern on the west coast.[13] The site is a small circular 'vitrified fort' only fifty feet across. One other such brooch, curiously similar, is known in Scotland, and came from the elaborately timber-laced fort at Castlelaw near Abernethy on the Tay (pl. 2a). These and some other sites across the centre of the country comprise what Childe called the *Abernethy complex*, and the possibility must now be taken seriously that this was formed in the third century rather than in the second as he once supposed. The still later dating which has recently been favoured,[14] was based, as Mrs Fowler has shown,[15] on the assumption that objects were brought to Scotland by refugees only at the end of their currency in England—as if refugees would be the only people to come north of the border. Further, the reassessment of the dates of Maiden Castle in Dorset has made the supposed Belgic date impossible for such a movement from southern England, even if the refugee theory were acceptable; La Tène Ic brooches at Maiden Castle, brought in by First B people, are now thought to occur throughout the third century B.C. but not longer.[16] Childe's suggestion that the Scottish examples are nearer to Swiss than English brooches has not been followed up.[17]

Another element in the complex, the peculiarly Scottish *crook pin*, which has the end of the ring turned outward, is more likely to have been, in the same way, a parallel development to the ring-headed pins of Southern Second A in Wessex than to have evolved further from them. Crook pins were found at Abernethy, at the Laws of Monifieth across the Tay—a very important site but complicated by a long later history—possibly in Clairinch in Loch Lomond, and at Bonchester near Hawick, where there was also part of a La Tène I/II iron fibula.[18] A complete brooch and three *ring-headed pins*, not crook pins, were found in the characteristically elongated vitrified fort of Dunagoil in Bute.[19] These ring-heads are English in type. One of them is cast but is otherwise very like another from Loch Moidart, a little north of Rahoy, which, in turn, is closely paralleled by another from Little Solsbury Hill in Somerset.[20] These ring-heads support Piggott's suggestion that Abernethy people arrived by the west coast; by contrast, the La Tène 1c brooches for which, as for the timber-lacing of the forts, a more directly Continental origin is possible, indicate an east-coast route. It is unlikely, however, that the 'complex' came ready-made; more probably it was brought about by arrivals who came by separate routes but who had some common background and language, and this process would continue over a period that may stretch back even to the beginnings of the sunflower pins —to judge from their central Scottish distribution. If spiral rings are removed from the Abernethy complex (see below) it may be called Second A, despite the presence of the two brooches. The type of timber-lacing may be earlier than classic *murus gallicus*, and not later, as Mrs Cotton supposed.[21]

Evolved *cast ring-headed pins* come down certainly to the second century or later,[22] such as one from Angus and a stray at Traprain with a solid head. One recorded from the island of Coll is of an Irish type, derived probably from Yorkshire, Eastern B. The absence of Eastern Second B types (Dane's Graves pins) from mainland Scotland may be significant, not only confirming the southern connections of what we have, but suggesting northward limits to Eastern B expansion.[23]

As already indicated, the certainty or probability of sites having *long*, though not necessarily continuous, *occupation* must always be remembered. For example, there is from Dunagoil a fragment of glass bangle datable to about 100 A.D.[24] Well-made iron-age sherds recently found at a site near Dunagoil[25] contrast with, and may be earlier than, the very poor pottery from the vitrified fort itself; this, in turn, resembles pottery from a supposed crannog in Bishop's Loch near Glasgow which also yielded an iron socketed axe. Dunagoil ware may have continued in the Clyde basin till Roman times. Pottery from Castlelaw, Abernethy, and from Finavon vitrified fort in Angus is somewhat similar, but there was no pottery at Rahoy. A fragment of a rotary quern indicates some late occupation at Finavon.

Increasing Iron-Age B Elements: second century B.C. to first century A.D.
That the Abernethy site itself was occupied at least down to the end of the second century B.C. is shown by the *spiral ring* which Mrs Piggott took to be an integral component of the Abernethy complex, and which, as she showed, represents an influx from the south into Scotland without touching central or northern England.[26] The origin was again Wessex or

Somerset. Jope has pointed out a distinction between wire and ribbon rings and has mapped further southern and south-eastern examples, the latter mainly of ribbon.[27] This Southern Second and Third B fondness for spiral finger and toe rings started a fashion that persisted in Scotland down to the eighth century, and the distribution at any period is still hard to map. Hamilton has recently adduced a severed hand wearing spiral rings, found at Gurness Broch in Orkney, as gruesome evidence of hostility between the broch people and the fort people further south.[28] A single early La Tène III brooch of South-western Third B origin comes from the Glenluce Sands in Wigtownshire.[29]

The Scottish type of *pin with projecting ring-head* must be distinguished from the foregoing pins although one comes from the multi-period Laws of Monifieth. Whether of bent wire or cast, this type is found widely over the mainland and in the islands, but it is so far not in evidence until the second century A.D. and thereafter has a long history.[30] A derivation either from sunflower pins or from southern involuted pins of the third to second century B.C. can now hardly be considered probable, except in the sense that a late survivor might have inspired someone who was familiar with south-western ring-heads still current in the first century A.D., for example at Meare in Somerset. If our projecting ring-heads were the result of the same move as introduced spiral rings, it is curious that there were none at the rich crannog at Hyndford in Lanarkshire, where the rings were common at about the end of the first century A.D.[31]

Quite a different distribution pattern is formed by the metal objects of finer quality, many of them freshly studied by Piggott in a series of papers published since the war. There are in Scotland not many pieces made before 50 A.D. and they all come from south of the central belt that is straddled by the 'Abernethy' finds. The two *sword chapes* from south-east Scotland and the scabbard from the English stretch of the Tweed, are dated by Piggott from late second to late first century B.C.[32] The Shaw Hill hoard from the centre of southern Scotland contained the famous highly decorated gold ring-terminal of a *torc* (in a fresh state), forty gold bullet-shaped *coins* of which the two survivors are well worn, and three gold torcs lost but recently republished.[33] Derek Allen ascribes the 'bullets' to the Marne-Aisne area of France and to the first half of the first century B.C., and dates, on coin evidence, the burial of the Snettisham (Norfolk) parallels to the terminal and torcs to about 25 B.C. or possibly earlier.[34] It seems unlikely that the Peeblesshire hoard should be much later. The 'bullets' are unique in Britain, unless a record of gold bullets at the fort of Dunnichen in Angus indicates more, as Daniel Wilson suggested.[35] British or Gaulish coins reached even Yorkshire to but a small

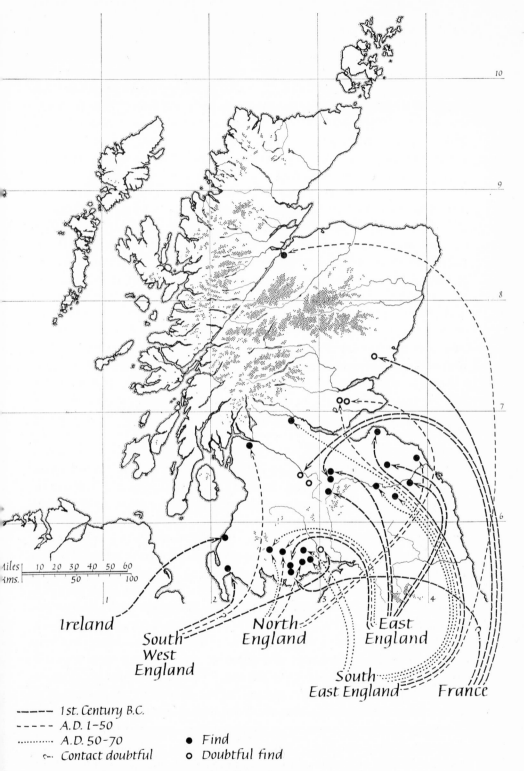

10

9

8

7

6

Miles | 10 20 30 40 50 60
Kms. | 50 100

1

2

3

4

Ireland

South
West
England

North
England

East
England

South
East England

France

–––– 1st. Century B.C.
---- A.D. 1–50
.... A.D. 50–70
⌐ Contact doubtful

● Find
○ Doubtful find

Fig. 2. Scottish finds and the contacts which they indicate.

extent and Allen records only two other possible finds in Scotland:[36] a Dobunnic gold stater that probably reached Dumfries in modern times, and an Armorican silver stater noted by Evans as from Lesmahagow in Lanarkshire, which is of a type that came into England about 50 B.C. and which is also recorded from Yorkshire and Northumberland. As the three scabbard finds and the hoard of torcs may all derive, according to Piggott and Fox,[37] from workshops somewhere between the Wash and south Yorkshire, they should represent contacts between southern Scotland and the Eastern Second B of England in the first century B.C.—the first noted in this survey and perhaps the indirect result of the pressure of Belgic expansion, and so really refugees.

The same contacts may surely be assumed to have brought to Kirkcudbrightshire, as a 150-year-old heirloom from the same area, the *Torrs* pony-cap and horns (pl. 1), hitherto familiar as a chamfrein.[38] The pleasing idea that it (or they) was made in south-west Scotland can hardly be maintained, and is unnecessary as evidence of a link for the Irish scabbard-style, which Jope now derives directly from the Continent and not Yorkshire.[39] The Continental increment in these first-century moves into Scotland, shown by the Marnian 'bullets' and perhaps the Armorican stater, may be responsible for the bronze buffer-ended *torc* from Kelton in Kirkcudbrightshire.[40] It has a movable segment that would be normal on elaborate foreign torcs but is curious on one so simple. An even simpler and smaller torc, turned into a bracelet, is unprovenanced from the Sim collection formed in Lanarkshire;[41] its very worn linear decoration might be rather earlier. Lastly, the Bargany *scabbard* may be an import into Ayrshire from northern Ireland, but, on Jope's reassessment, not necessarily earlier than Piggott's late first century B.C.[42]

The map of things made in the *first century A.D.* is better filled, but must be subdivided in order to distinguish between earlier imports and objects that came north or were made in the north as a result of the Roman occupation of Brigantia, soon after 70 A.D., and of the Agricolan advance ten years later. With the exception of a few brooches, and perhaps the Deskford boar's head, these are again confined to southern Scotland.

There are the large crescent of sheet bronze and the rectangular strip from *Balmaclellan* in Kirkcudbrightshire, decorated in good 'mirror style' like that of southern England, which Fox would date to about 30 or 40 A.D. and ascribe to northern or eastern England;[43] they are part of a set of curiously shaped plates and cannot be shield mounts. With them was hidden an actual *mirror* in a later style ascribed by Hawkes to Yorkshire just before the occupation.[44] A rather dim reflection of the mirror style is found on one of the presumably ritual *spoons* found with an inhumation at Burnmouth, Berwickshire, as on the pair from Crosby Ravensworth in Westmorland, and unlike the decoration of the other spoons of the kind in southern England, Wales and Ireland;[45] they might be mid-century. Better and perhaps slightly earlier curvilinear decoration comes from *Langbank* crannog in the Clyde, on a small bone comb; from the same site there is a buffer-ended penannular brooch which if of the same date, or even earlier, would be the earliest associated penannular in Scotland (pl. 2a).[46] What may be examples of a north British type of *mirror-handle*, baluster shaped, come from the Carlingwark Loch hoard, submerged perhaps late in the century, and from an unknown provenance.[47]

Contacts with Iron Age C. With the first century A.D. there seems to begin the direct influence of south-east, Belgic, Britain on Scotland which Piggott identified.[48] To the La Tène II derivative *brooch* that he found in a fort near North Berwick[49] may be added a brooch of the type that Hull has named after Colchester which was found outside the Rink fort near Selkirk,[50] and a Langton Down fibula, a type commonest in Claudian times, apparently found about 1833 with a spearhead when a tumulus with burials of unknown date was destroyed near Merlsford, Strathmiglo, Fife.[51] Another Claudian brooch, resembling the Aucissa type, actually got up to Dores near Inverness.[52] Made perhaps soon after 50 A.D. are the *enamelled cheekpiece* from Eckford, Roxburghshire, probably East British, and two Belgic pieces found in Kirkcudbrightshire, the tankard handle from the Carlingwark hoard and the enamelled *terret* from Auchendolly.[53] There is also a fine Polden Hill brooch with open-work catchplate from Polmaise near Stirling.[54]

The Roman Advance. These then, and the cauldrons and cauldron-chains found in the Carlingwark and Blackburn Mill, Berwickshire, *hoards* mark in some manner affiliations between the Scottish Iron Age and Belgic and allied cultures.[55] Derek Allen's demonstration that the coins previously assumed to be Brigantian are in fact Coritanian emphasises the lateness of significant south-eastern influences, even in Yorkshire.[56] It seems likely that the distant scattering of the brooches represents a move northwards ahead of the Roman army but that the bulk of the south-eastern objects from the hoards come later, perhaps, as Piggott suggested, in the course of military corn imports; for the alternative idea of a coastal trade in pre-Roman times is hard to believe, particularly if it came to Scotland while by-passing Brigantia.[57] For during more than a century southern Scotland had been increasingly assimilated to northern England, on the evidence of the other metal-work, producing a Third B culture.

IANB C

With the Roman advance there comes a sharp rise in the number and variety of objects to be studied. The new types are found both on Roman and native sites. A group of 'Brigantian' *scabbards* and *sword-guards* extending into Scotland and dating from mid-first into the second century A.D. was isolated by Piggott.[58] The fine Mortonhall scabbard from near Edinburgh has been shown by cleaning to have been enhanced by a contrast between the golden bronze of the applied loop and strap with open-work, and the sheath itself which is more copper-coloured. On the fighting effectiveness of this group it may be commented that into this Mortonhall scabbard, which Piggott thought too thin for use, can be fitted the blade of one from first-century Newstead which was indeed used, but proved deficient: for after the sword's little crown-shaped bronze guard had been notched by two Roman strokes the blade buckled.[59]

Another type of object, the *beaded torc*, probably belonged in part to the pre-Roman phase. Its distribution is more markedly western than the others.[60] There are considerable variations in style and doubtless in date. The finest is from Lochar Moss, Dumfriesshire, while that from Lamberton Moor, Berwickshire, is typologically the last. One comes from Hyndford crannog in the Clyde valley, a site particularly important because of the relatively large number of finds from it and because its flourishing period appears restricted to a generation or so around 100 A.D.: it contained a fair amount of Flavian samian but perhaps only one sherd of Antonine pottery,[61] although close to the Roman fort of Castledykes occupied in both periods. More possibly accidental was the absence as already noted of pins when there were three spiral rings and a sophisticated buffer-ended penannular brooch. The absence from all the crannogs of bone *weaving-combs* was noted by Childe.

These combs have a very curious distribution. Despite the emphasis that has been placed on their occurrence in South-western B they are at home in Iron-Age A, B, and C contexts in England and even last on there into Roman times though mainly in the north.[62] West Yorkshire caves and Borness cave in Kirkcudbrightshire provide first-to-second-century A.D. contexts. The other south Scottish examples are from two Roman forts, first-century Newstead and second-century Camelon. Traprain indeed has no surviving bone objects but the negative evidence of other native sites seems significant. Nothing suggests that they are pre-Roman in Scotland. Then there is a jump to the wheel-houses of the Hebrides and the brochs of the north. There is no obvious interpretation, but it seems wrong to deduce an Iron Age B origin for the northern 'culture' mainly from these combs. If Borness is intermediate one must note that its series of curious bone toggles is now paralleled in late Belgic Cambridgeshire.[63]

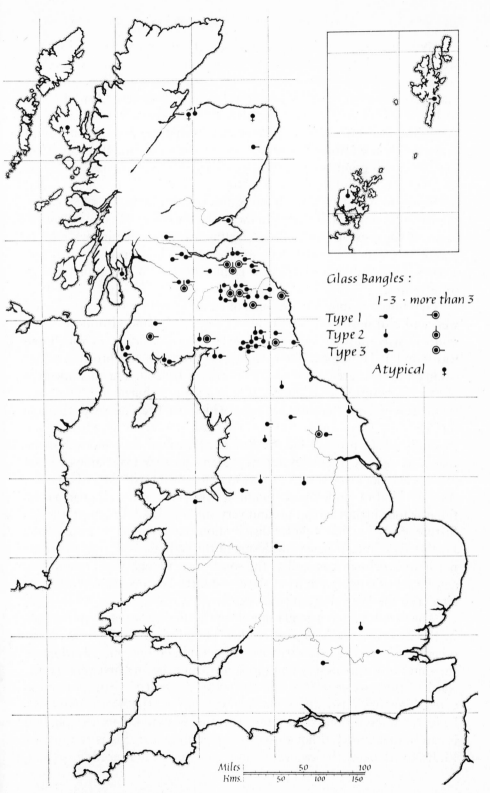

Glass Bangles :

1–3 · more than 3

Type 1

Type 2

Type 3

Atypical

Miles
Kms.

Fig. 3. Distribution of glass bangles.

Hyndford was rich in *glass bangles*, particularly ice-green with blue and white inlaid cords like a piece found in a first-century level at Newstead.[64] There was no previous British tradition of these, and they may have been trade goods produced by some Romanised Gaul for sale within the frontier. Considering that the first-century frontier lay in Perthshire and Angus,[65] it is curious that the natives immediately south of it scarcely used them. There may have been some forcible evacuation, but this distribution combines with the evidence of brooches and dress-fasteners, and with that of the pre-Roman metal-work, to suggest a real difference in population north and south of the Forth. To a less extent there is a difference in intensity in the bangle distribution between south-east and south-west Scotland, the south-eastern predominance making a contrast with the exclusively south-western incidence of first- and second-century crannogs,[66] which cannot be due to the availability of watery sites.

Hyndford crannog is in the area of cultural overlap between east and west and also north and south; for the south-east and also most of the south-west is quite devoid of the *stone cup-shaped lamps*, of which one was found at Hyndford. They occur in souterrains and brochs and are common in their areas, as well as in northern Ireland. The identification of them as lamps is based on the frequent signs of burning.[67] There is a strong resemblance to a Roman lamp which has been misused, the hole for the wick becoming a thumb-hold, and it may be doubted if any example will turn out to be pre-Roman: Dunagoil once more must be treated as equivocal, but development seems possible from lamps formed of shapeless hollowed stones such as were found at Castlelaw, Abernethy. Another kind of stone object found at Hyndford is the circular *palette* three or four inches across, ground very smooth. Like the lamps it needs further study but has a wider distribution than they have south of the Forth-Clyde line. It is very widespread throughout Scotland, including northern broch-sites as well as the south-east, though the Traprain ex-amples when datable are from third-to-fourth-century contexts. Childe cited also the West Yorkshire caves.[68]

The bangle map is a good example of the dominance of Traprain Law in the Scottish *archaeological record*. Traprain's early iron-age finds, other than from the very early overlap period and one pin, all belong to the times of its greatest extent (40 acres) from the late first century on-wards;[69] the 20-acre area within the upper rampart is virtually unexca-vated. This obviously affects our knowledge, and the Scottish archaeo-logical record is seriously unbalanced in other ways too. Another oppidum is rarely mentioned although its extent is 39 acres: this is the one on Eildon overlooking the major Roman site of Newstead near Melrose, and,

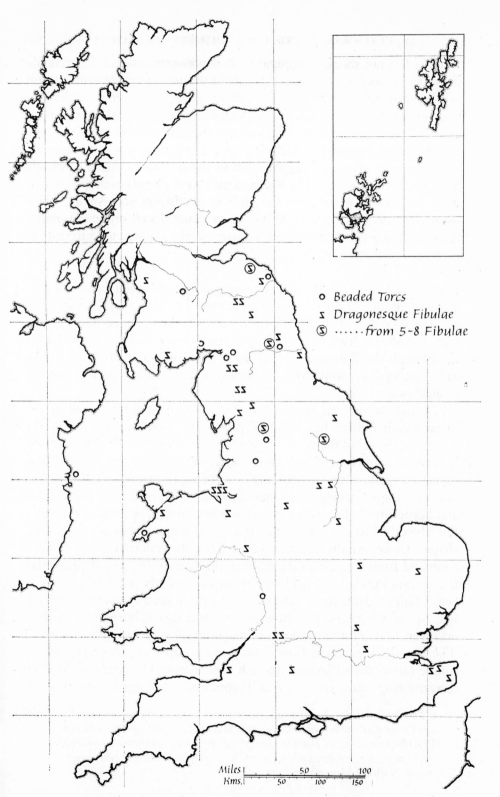

o Beaded Torcs
ʃ Dragonesque Fibulae
Ⓢ ·······from 5-8 Fibulae

Miles
Kms.
50   100
50   100   150

Fig. 4. Distribution of beaded torcs and dragonesque fibulae.

whether or not its main occupation was pre-Roman, no real understanding of the Iron Age in southern Scotland is surely possible until Eildon can be brought into the story.[70] The same applies to the smaller but strategic site at Birrenswark in Dumfriesshire, past which the 'chamfrein' and the mirror and the rest must have come into the south-west. There is also a particular need for following up earlier excavations and accidental discoveries by systematic exploration of those districts that historically have been the heartlands of Scotland and were already well covered by early bronze-age graves, the lowlands of Perthshire and Angus, Aberdeenshire and Moray, from which the number of well preserved monuments in the less intensively settled parts of the country tend to distract archaeological attention.

The Second Century A.D. Traprain seems to have flourished continuously throughout the Flavian (*c.* 80-100) and Antonine (*c.* 140-190) occupations and the Trajanic-Hadrianic interval between them, suggesting that the local Votadini at least were friendly to the Romans and did not suffer for it, although the Roman army was heavily engaged notably around 100, 117, 130, 140, 155 and 185.[71] Culturally at any rate the period must be treated as a whole.

Dress-fasteners and dragonesque brooches are prominent among the items which Gillam has listed as part of the common culture of the Romano-Britons of the northern military province.[72] Both share the new fashion of enamelling in several colours, not just in red as earlier. They repeat the pattern set by the bangles in being primarily suited to native taste but found largely on Roman garrison sites from York northwards and bordering Wales, with a scatter southward and, in these two cases, a few abroad. The fasteners, with triangular loops and heads of various shapes, are apparently descended from a South-western B double-headed form and from ring-heads included in the remarkable sets of Brigantian horse-trappings (*c.* 70 A.D.) from Stanwick, recently published in full at last.[73] Gillam dates those with disc and square heads, generally enamelled, to the Hadrianic-Antonine period, and this is borne out by their occurrence at Traprain where there were moulds for casting them.[74] The usually unenamelled boss-and-petal group may, however, be Antonine rather than Flavian although absent from Hadrian's Wall. Plain disc and ring-heads continued at Traprain into the third-to-fourth-cen-

---

*Pl. 3a Two bridle-bits for chariot ponies, with enamelled ornament (red and probably another colour) from Birrenswark and with bosses from Middlebie, both Dumfriesshire (p. 31).
(b) Terrets, rein-rings, of 'Donside' type (p. 32), from Cairngryffe fort, Lanarkshire, from Towie, Aberdeenshire (pair), from Clova, Aberdeenshire and Kirriemuir, Angus.
(Photos. National Museum of Antiquities)*

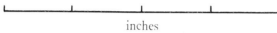

inches

inches

inches

Pl. 4. Boar's head from Deskford, Banffshire (p. 32),
probably the mouth of a war-trumpet (carnyx).
(Photo. National Museum of Antiquities)

turies. The attractive dragonesque brooches fully illustrated by Feachem, seem to have flourished particularly about the second quarter of the second century.[75]

Perhaps early in the second century the hoard found at Lamberton in Berwickshire (pl. 2b) was buried, with its late beaded torc, enamelled dragonesque and head-stud brooches, spiral rings and Roman paterae.[76] It also contained several small lathe-worked bronze *bowls* that are not Roman. A simpler bowl was found with the Lochar Moss beaded-torc. Jope has recently assigned to southern English workshops both lathe-cleaned and fully spun bowls found in Ireland, but the technique could have spread.[77] The embossed bands of the Lamberton bowls which recur at Stanwick,[78] are reminiscent of the embossed decoration on the cauldron from Kincardine Moss near Stirling[79] and of the domed rivet-heads on bowls from south-western England, including Glastonbury lake-village.[80] Without wishing to press the idea or forgetting the ornamental rivet-heads of the Mortonhall scabbard, one may wonder if there is a connection between such embossed knobs and the development of the generally cast *boss-style* of North Britain south of the Forth, best seen in the Middlebie hoard from the district of Birrenswark (pl. 3a). Curle's dating of boss-style ornaments including fasteners at Newstead is unfortunately not clear, but may be read as ascribing them to the Antonine barracks.[81] It is not clear whether the bosses on the larger Middlebie bridle-bit in that hoard are typologically a replacement of, or parallel to, the enamelled panels on the well-known Birrenswark bit, both evolved from the late Brigantian form of bit found at Stanwick.[82]

Alongside the *ring-headed* pins, already discussed on p. 21, there appears a class of pin with a kind of turned-back snout for a head, the *zoomorphic* pin, and the zoomorphic penannular brooch with similar terminals. The pins were found at Traprain and one each at Roman Newstead and at Covesea cave in Morayshire. The brooch distribution is wider and includes Wales. This suggests a product of Gillam's cultural province, developing in a small way during the second century but of importance for the future.[83]

We now turn to objects showing a strong local development of fine metal-work north of the Forth and Clyde, indicating a gathering of strength and a growing cultural unity there during the century following Mons Graupius. Heavy penannular *bronze armlets*, like those from the entrance of a souterrain at Castle Newe, Aberdeenshire (pl. 5b), are basically a north-east Scottish class that occurs twice between the Roman Walls and once in Co. Down. Piggott has drawn attention to the resemblance between the design of the armlets and the ring and lips of the Shaw Hill gold terminal.[84] Another element in the design, as J. A. Smith saw long ago, is a rod tightly bent into a z-shaped snake and then curved in on itself.[85] One armlet, formerly at Glamis Castle, seems to have had the edges of the rod free, in part at least.[86] The rest are cast solid, and later still the z-pattern was lost; some of this final group have very exaggerated lips. Yellow and red enamel occasionally survives in the openings at the ends, once resembling the chequer pattern on a dress-fastener found at Drumashie near Inverness along with an enamelled belt-plate on which there is trumpet-shaped decoration related to the rudimentary lips of the 'Glamis' armlet. The belt-plate and dress-fastener may well be imports to the north.[87] All these pieces are cast, unlike the possibly earlier boar's head from *Deskford* in Banffshire with cognate repoussé ornament, which Piggott has recently discussed fully and identified as the mouth of a carnyx or trumpet (pl. 4).[88]

With one of the armlets was found a spiral *snake-bracelet*.[89] By far the finest and heaviest of this class is from the Culbin Sands, Morayshire (pl. 5a). Most come from Angus, including one from a souterrain and two newly found in a probable broch.[90] Another recent find is from Skye[91] and there is one from south of the Forth. Several of the best, or earliest, of these bracelets retain a pattern along the spine which is a more or less remote cast derivative of the chased wavy line that is seen on the only known ancestral example, from the immediately pre-Roman grave at Snailwell in Cambridgeshire; Lethbridge noted the similar punched detail on a torc or girdle from late first-century Newstead.[92]

The range in size and quality of these two kinds of rather baroque ornaments suggests immigrant bronze-smiths and local imitators over several generations. There is no positive evidence for a date for any of them later than the second century. The two distributions correspond reasonably well with the souterrains clustered in Angus and Perthshire, western Aberdeenshire and Sutherland. The armlet found at Stanhope near the head of the Tweed, of developed though not exaggerated type, was found with two boss-style ornaments and a Roman patera that might be as late as the end of the century.[93] The one from Roxburghshire was unearthed at or near the find-spot of the Stichill hinged collar,[94] the largest and most sophisticated piece ascribed to the boss style; the bosses are repoussé, while the tendril decoration in relief on much thicker metal is tooled or engraved, not cast, resembling some Irish finds (pl. 6).[95]

Lastly there are the bronze *terrets* (pl. 3b) with iron bars in their

---

Pl. 5a Spiral bracelet from Culbin Sands, Moray (p. 32) with a stylised human head at either end; note the blue glass inset eye and the setting for a disc, probably of red enamel as mouth, and the hair on the back of the head. (b) Heavy armlet (p. 31), one of a pair from a souterrain at Castle Newe, Aberdeenshire. The inset red and yellow chequered enamel disc is held by iron pins.) Photos. National Museum of Antiquities and British Museum)

inches

inch

inches

Pl. 6 Jointed collar from Stichill, Roxburghshire (p. 32).
(Photo. National Museum of Antiquities)

sockets, named by Kilbride-Jones after the Aberdeenshire river Don, which spread southwards beyond the armlets and bracelets as far as Wales and Northamptonshire.[96] Piggott has suggested that they derive from a Roman military type.[97] The evidence for date is meagre but in view of the distribution, general style and fondness for weight, one must

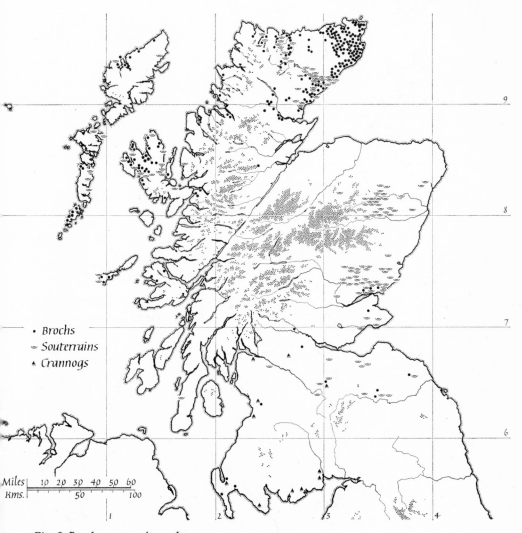

Fig. 6. Brochs, souterrains and crannogs.

prefer something earlier than Alcock's Dark Age proposal,[98] such as Piggott's suggestion that they mark the trail of the *Caledonian alliance* which swept over Hadrian's Wall about 197 A.D. and probably combined

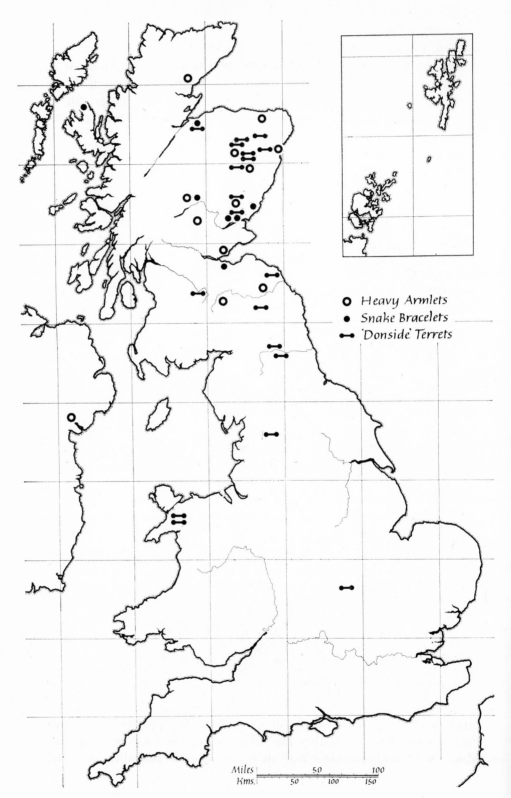

Fig. 5. *Distribution of heavy armlets, snake bracelets and 'Donside' terrets.*

Heavy Armlets
Snake Bracelets
'Donside' Terrets

with a general rising further south.[99] This tremendous event destroyed Traprain for at least a generation, and led to settlement of south-eastern Scotland by souterrain builders, probably the Maeatae of history, from Angus and beyond.

Souterrains north of the Tay have yielded second-century Roman pottery as well as a late-second to third-century imported brooch.[100] But some of those south of the Forth were built of abandoned Roman second-century stones, at Newstead and at Crichton near Edinburgh, and Richmond has suggested that the Roman tombstones built, at Skirva near Kirkintilloch, into the ditch of the Antonine Wall itself had formed part of another.[101] Accepting the discovery of probable broch sites in Angus, Fife and West Lothian by the Royal Commission's staff and their confirmation of others, it seems to the writer more than a coincidence that the rare *brochs* south of the Tay are, in four instances, situated only a few miles from the rare south-eastern souterrains. Three in Angus along the Tay also mark this alliance of northern and eastern tribes.

This conclusion agrees with the southern trickle of ornaments and with the second-century date of the cock-shaped brooch found at Bow broch, Midlothian;[102] but it conflicts with the conclusions reached by Curle, and later by Piggott, as to the date of *Torwoodlee* broch nearby. However, first-century Roman sherds from under the broch wall, some belonging to the same pots as on the floor in the centre, should indicate an earlier rather than a contemporary deposit, and Harden would have liked some clear glass to be second century.[103] Further, there was a flat rotary quern lying in the bottom of a ditch of the earlier fort, which had become well silted up before the broch ditch was cut. This is not easy to reconcile with a broch date as early as 100 to 130, because the first-century native querns found at Roman Newstead and native sites in eastern Scotland are high beehives, though a flat grinding surface had also been developed. It is possible to reconcile the difficulties and explain the short life of the broch before its destruction, which Piggott demonstrated, if the broch builders came as invaders soon after 197 or 186 (assuming the Antonine Wall to be abandoned by then), and were ejected by Severus' great punitive campaign in 209 onwards.

Epilogue. The scale and thoroughness with which the *pax Romana* was then imposed, to give peace on the frontier for a century, was asserted some years ago,[104] and has been borne out by further excavation of the military sites.[105] It is significant and sinister that we have no further fine metal-work to study. There was no new art style in the north-east: perhaps the warrior aristocracy had met its Culloden; nor was there a return to old ways even in the south. *Traprain* seems to have made a slow re-

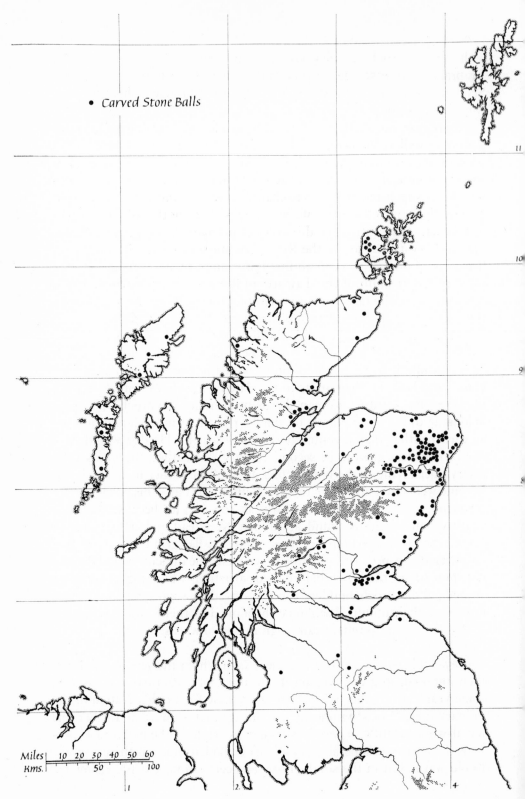

• Carved Stone Balls

Miles 10 20 30 40 50 60
Kms. 50 100

Fig. 7. Distribution of carved stone balls (after D. M. Marshall).

covery. There is a gap in the coin series there between 155 and 250.[106] The Roman pottery, however, needs re-examination to see if it also supports the idea of a long break, which is favoured by Feachem less than by Mrs Fowler.[107] She confirms that the main stratigraphical division of the site occurs at this time and notes that in the interval the boss-style vanished, 'presumably because there was no continuing demand for such trappings'. The later third and the fourth century were Traprain's most flourishing period as a town friendly to Rome. Home products were then evidently less attractive than the ordinary Romano-British objects which were commonly imported—coins, pottery, glass and gadgets.[108] There was an echo of the boss-style in the new rosette and 'proto-hand' *pins* made on the spot and there was some development of the *zoomorphic brooch* on the terminals of which enamelling was just kept alive, but native inventiveness seems to have been restricted and unambitious.[109] One might say that the Early Iron Age had petered out, but also that the growth of the Late Iron Age of the post-Roman world had begun.[110]

Those pins and brooches were to be developed into the lovely silver pins and the great decorated brooches of the seventh and eighth centuries,[111] and the cultural divisions we have been noting became those of the early historical kingdoms. When the Anglo-Saxons conquered south-eastern Scotland in the seventh century Strathclyde survived as British, and the Picts stretched north from the Forth as their sculptured monuments show archaeologically.[112] Now that the evidence favours a neolithic or early bronze-age date for the carved stone balls,[113] Childe's comparison of their distribution to that of Pictish sculpture[114] hints at ancient differences continuing to underlie the movements we have been considering.

Notes

1. Where references to publications are not given they will generally be found in V. G. Childe, *Prehistory of Scotland* (1935).
2. *PSAS* XCIII (1959-60), 16-134. For distribution of ornaments *cit*. map 7, and V. B. Proudfoot, *Downpatrick Gold Find* (1955) fig. 5.
3. *PSAS* XCII (1958-9), 1-9.
4. *Ant. J* XXXVII (1957), 159-60; *Yorks. AJ* CLXII (1964), etc. Flat-rimmed pottery as generally discussed should be susceptible of divisions that reflect long development and degrees of outside influence, e.g. the introduction of sandy temper that dominates at Old Keig. It is unlikely that Highland Zone clay is really responsible for similarities, for very varied but typical neolithic and bronze-age fabrics were made of it; nor is bad pottery of other traditions similar.

5. *Aspects of Archaeology*, ed. W. F. Grimes (1951), 214-19, figs. 55-7.

6. *Staple Howe* (1963), 61-2.

7. Cf. *Arch. Camb.* CVIII (1960), 127. Calf of Eday, Orkney: *PSAS* LXXIII (1938-9), 182.

8. J. R. C. Hamilton, *Jarlshof* (1956), 32-3, 36. The repeated confusion starts with Curle, for he gives two find-spots for the mould for a bronze sword, which provided his best evidence that the bronze-smith continued to work in 'Village II', and the most circumstantially stated spot is in 'Village I', being at a level well below the hearth of the later period (*PSAS* LXVIII (1933-4), 240 and 281). Other fragments of the mould evidently really were found higher, but there must have been disturbance of the bronze-working level as the First A people dug our earliest souterrain through it (ibid., 237).

9. Few of the significant 'Village I' sherds seem to have been securely stratified. Slag: *PSAS* LXVIII (1933-4), 303; this might have been intrusive from 'Village II', or might be bronze-working refuse, for iron-slag may be deceptive in this connection (R. F. Tylecote, *Metallurgy in Archaeology* (1962), 34).

10. *PSAS* LXXX (1945-6), 149-50.

11. *PSAS* LXXXIX (1955-6), 129-30, 211. Mrs Fowler misreads Childe, *Scotland before the Scots* (1946), 81, in supposing that he lists socketed axes from Dunagoil, Monifieth, etc.; those are shaft-hole axes.

12. *Arch. J* LXXXV (1928), 170-5, *JRSAI* LXXIV (1944), 36.

13. *PSAS* LXXII (1937-8), 38-40. La Tène 1c brooches: *Arch. J* CX (1953), 93.

14. Starting with *Scotland before the Scots* cit. 129; cf. *PSAS* LXXXIX (1955-6), 129.

15. *PPS* XXVI (1960), 161.

16. *Ant.* XXXIII (1959), 179-80.

17. As note 13. For comments on their hinge mechanism, *PPS* XXVI (1960), 163.

18. *PPS* XXI (1955), 288-9; *PSAS* LXXXIV (1949-50), 122, 130; possible Welsh example, W. Gardner and H. N. Savory, *Dinorben* (1964), 131.

19. *T Bute NHS* IX (1925), pl. 41; *PSAS* LXXXIV (1949-50), 130 ill.

20. Eignaig, Inverness-shire: *PSAS* LVI (1921-2), 21-3. Solsbury; *Arch J* XCI (1934), 275 ill.

21. *Arch. J* CXI (1954), 58-9. *Germania*, 1960, 43 ff.

22. Inverkeillor, Angus: Nat. Mus. Ants. Scot. Catalogue, FC 145. Traprain: *PSAS* LVI (1921-2), 215, fig. 15. Coll: *PSAS* XV (1880-1), 81, fig. 3; cf. *Problems of the Iron Age in S. Britain*, 80.

23. I. M. Stead, *La Tène Cultures of E. Yorkshire* (1965), 56-9. A pin like those from Ireland ill. in *Arch. J* XCI (1934), 285, nos. 2 and 3 has however been found in 1962 on the southern side of the Cheviots. I am indebted to

Mr Jobey for this information; High Knowes, *Arch. Ael.*, forthcoming.

24. *T Bute NHS* IX (1925), 59; *PSAS* LXXXVIII (1954-6), 210, fig. 1.6.

25. *T Bute NHS* XVI (1964), 18, 'Little Dunagoil'.

26. *PSAS* LXXXIV (1949-50), 132ff.

27. *UJA* XX (1957), 79-81.

28. *Northern Isles*, ed. F. T. Wainwright (1962), 64. Ring at Clickhimin Broch, Shetland: ibid., 81. Except for Castlelaw Abernethy, all the Scottish mainland examples come from sites that have also yielded pottery or objects of the Roman period: Castlehaven, Lochlee, Hyndford, Gallanach, Monifieth, Carpow (*Ill. Lond. News* 29.9.1962), Granton (D. Wilson, *Archaeol. & Prehistoric Annals of Scotland* (1851), 327), Traprain, Lamberton, Newstead, Edgerston (R.C.A.H.M., *Roxburghshire* (1956), 228). Much later survivals: Buston and Norrie's Law.

29. Fragment with external cord, unpublished in Nat. Mus. Ants., cf. Bulleid and Gray, *Glastonbury* (1911), 192-3 and pl. xl, E 185 with refs. to Hunsbury, Northants.

30. *PPS* XXI (1955), 288. ibid. XXVI (1960), 163.

31. See below, p. 26.

32. *PPS* XVI (1950), 11ff.

33. The identification as a sceptre-head and the name Cairnmuir are both superseded: *PSAS* XCI (1957-8), 112-16. The terminal is composed of almost 21 carat gold; spectrographic analysis, 85 per cent gold, 9 per cent silver, 3·5 per cent copper, 2·5 per cent iron, with a trace of tin: *Arch. J* CVI (1949), 60n. The recorded weights of the torcs (*Arch. Scotica* IV (1857), 217-19) show that the old drawing was not full size and suggest a diameter of about $6\frac{1}{2}$ ins. for the loop terminal torcs rather than $3\frac{1}{2}$. For the recent brass facsimile based on the drawing and illustrated in *PSAS* cit., pl. xi.2 weighs 20·65 gms. and the torc 'of uncommon fineness' 267·5 gms. (8 oz. 12 dwt.), and assuming the specific gravity of the gold at 18 and of the brass at 8·7, the dimensions of the facsimile should be multiplied by

$$\sqrt{\frac{267\cdot5}{20\cdot65} \times \frac{8\cdot7}{18}} = \sqrt[3]{6\cdot24} = 1\cdot84.$$

I am indebted to I. H. Longworth and Professor Kemmer for the mathematics involved.

34. *Problems of the Iron Age in S. Britain*, 'bullets', 104, 170; Snettisham, 111, 122-3.

35. *Archaeol. and Prehist. Annals* (1851), 520.

36. *Problems of the Iron Age in S. Britain*, 256, 273.

37. C. Fox, *Pattern and Purpose* (1958), 45.

38. *Arch.* XCVI (1955), 197-235. I find it hard to believe that they were not made up as one object in antiquity.

39. *Problems of the Iron Age in S. Britain*, 79; *UJA* XVII (1954), 81-91.

40. *PSAS* LXXXII (1947-8), 293-5: there ascribed in error to the Kelton in Dumfriesshire.

41. *Nat. Mus. Ants. Cat.* DO 22.

42. *UJA* XVII (1954), 87-91.

43. Fox, *Pattern and Purpose*, 116.

44. *Ant. J* XX (1940), 349.

45. *PSAS* LVIII (1923-4), 143-51; add *Ant. J* XIII (1933), 464.

46. *T Glasgow AS* V (1902-6), 46; R. Munro, *Archaeology and False Antiquities* (1905), pl. xii. The brooch is of a variety that starts in Iron Age A, cf. R. E. M. Wheeler, *Maiden Castle* (1934), fig. 86.1, but has grooving on the pin as ibid., fig. 86.5 (first century A.D.). Mrs Fowler's classification in *PPS* XXVI (1960), 149ff. is hard to apply, and she calls the Maiden Castle brooch Aa, despite its decorated terminals, but the Langbank one A3iii (pp. 172 and 175). The plainer brooches of type Aa cannot in Scotland be dated early just on the strength of occurrence at the Laws of Monifieth (p. 161): the one from Craigie (also in Angus) was associated with a projecting ring-head pin.

47. Carlingwark: *PSAS* LXXXVII (1952-3), 1ff. Handles: Fox, *Pattern and Purpose*, 99; add *UJA* XVII (1954), 93. No provenance: Nat. Mus. Ants. 'FG 8', but it is not known why this has replaced the ring illustrated by D. Wilson as coming from Merlsford (note 51 below).

48. *PSAS* LXXXVII (1952-3), 17-19.

49. *PSAS* XCI (1957-8), 70-4.

50. This type is the predecessor of the head-stud brooch with which J. Curle identified it, *PSAS* LXVI (1931-2), 367. Brooch typology: Hawkes and Hull, *Camulodunum* (1947), 308ff.

51. Nat. Mus. Ants. FG 1. Merlsford: *Arch. Scotica* V (1890), App. 25 (1833); O.S. 6-inch map Fife Sheet 16 (1856). The record is confused for neither the spearhead FG2 nor the ring (note 47 above) are the same as in D. Wilson, loc. cit.

52. *PSAS* LXVI (1931-2), 395.

53. *PSAS* LXXXVII (1952-3), 12, 20-2, 30; XCI (1957-8), 74n.

54. *PSAS* LXVI (1931-2), 336-7, 385.

55. *PSAS* XCI (1957-8), 74. The Blackburn Mill patera could be mid-first century (*Ant. J* XLI (1961), 25) rather than mid-second (*PSAS* LXXXVII (1952-3), 50). Plough-shares must now be excluded from these connections; the shares and spades have been reassessed by A. Fenton, ibid., XCVI (1962-3), 269-73.

56. D. F. Allen, *Coins of the Coritani* (Sylloge of Coins of the British Isles), 1963.

57. *PSAS* LXXXVII (1952-3), 19, and XCI (1957-8), 74.

58. *PPS* XVI (1950), 17-21.

59. J. Curle, *A Roman Frontier Post—Newstead* (1911), 185.

60. *PSAS* LXXXII (1947-8), 294—add Lambay Island *PRIA* XXXVIII (1928-9), 243, mid-first century (*Ant. J* XX (1940), 347). Lochar Moss: *Arch.* XXXIV (1852), 83-7, Fox, *Pattern and Purpose*, pl. 29.

61. *PSAS* LXVI (1931-2), 381-2; finds now in Nat. Mus. Ants. The coarse sherds were kindly examined by Mr Gillam and Mr Hartley, cf. A. S. Roberston, *Roman Fort at Castledykes* (1964).

62. *Maiden Castle*, 297-8; Bulleid and Gray, *Meare Lake Village* I (1948), 61-71; *PPS* XVI (1950), 146-7, 160.

63. *P Cambridge AS* XLVII (1953), 31-32. At Stanwick in bronze, *PPS* XXVIII (1962), 41, fig. 6.

64. *PSAS* LXXII (1937-8), 366-95, and LXXXVIII (1954-6), 208-21 (add Type I from Tentsmuir, Fife in Dunfermline Museum). *Ant.* XXXVI (1962), 237.

65. *PSAS* LXXIV (1939-40), 45; *Roman and Native in North Britain*, ed. I. A. Richmond (1958), 54.

66. *PSAS* LXXXVII (1952-3), 148-51.

67. Re-examination of 78 examples in Nat. Mus. Ants. by I. H. Longworth gives 39 as burnt internally, 18 indefinite (including 6 burnt externally only), 21 no signs of burning, despite Steer's contention that only 4 out of 75 are burnt—*PSAS* LXXXIX (1955-6), 243-6. The lamps from Okstrow, Orkney, are cognate—Childe, *Prehistory of Scotland*, 248 ill.

68. To his list (*Prehistory of Scotland*, 245) add for southern Scotland, Birrens Roman Fort, Dumfriesshire, also McCulloch's Castle, Kircudbrightshire (*TD and GNHAS* XLI (1962-3), 123). West Yorks: in Brit. Mus. from Longcliffe Scar and Dowkerbottom; also Kirkhead Cave, Ulverston, Lancs.: *Mems. Anthrop. Soc. London* 11 (1865-6), 360.

69. Metal-work: *PSAS* LXXXIX (1955-6), 118-221. Plan: ibid., 284-9.

70. R.C.A.H.M., *Roxburghshire*, 18, 23ff., 306-10.

71. Ibid., 23-30; *Roman and Native*, chaps. ii-iii.

72. *Roman and Native*, 82.

73. Ibid., 79-85, 90. Stanwick: *PPS* XXVIII (1962), 17-57, esp. 23 for additions to Gillam's list.

74. *PSAS* LXXXIX (1955-6), 181.

75. Ibid., 159. *Ant. J* XVIII (1938), 146ff. and ibid., XXXI (1951), 32-44.

76. *PSAS* XXXIX (1904-5), 367-76 and LXVI (1931-2), 363-4; and above, p. 26.

77. *UJA* XX (1957), 85-6, cf. *Ant. J* XLI (1961), 191ff. Lochar Moss bowl illustrated: Wilson: *Arch. and Prehistoric Annals*, 1851, pl. III.

78. *PPS* XXVIII (1962), 29.

79. *PSAS* XIX (1884-5), 313; omitted from the major modern studies of cauldrons this vessel has been dated to the seventh century B.C. (Rynne,

J Galway AHS XXIX (1960), 1-2) and first century A.D. (Piggott, *PSAS* LXXXVII (1952-3), 13).

80. *Glastonbury*, I, 179-82.

81. *Newstead*, 302-5.

82. E. T. Leeds, *Celtic Ornament* (1933), 115-16; *PPS* V (1939), 183 and XXVIII (1962), 23. It has been argued (*PPS* XXIX (1963), 209-10) that bits with rein-rings and end-links cast solid, as at Stanwick and earlier, were not functional but ritual imitations. In particular that from Birrenswark (overall 9·2 ins. wide compared with 10·1 for the smallest from Stanwick), though the rings are much worn and indeed repaired, is said to be too small for the smallest pony. Mr J. G. Speed of the Royal (Dick) Veterinary College, however, tells me that the Britons in the Early Iron Age made use of cross-breeding to get more slender and shorter ponies, reducing their height from *c.* 12 hands like Exmoor ponies to *c.* 11 like the modern Welsh mountain pony. The narrower jaws would need a reduction in the width of the bit, and the three-link type would have ceased to exert sufficient control if the fusion of rings and end-links had not taken place. Two points of wear (centres 1·3 ins. apart) on the back of the Birrenswark bit press on the front lower molars of such a jaw, and the wear on the links occurs at the right places also.

83. *PSAS* LXXXIX (1955-6), 137-9, 164-72 and *Arch. J* CXX (1963), 98-160; *PPS* XXVI (1960), 167-9 and XXI (1955), 289-92; *PRIA* XLIII (1935-7), 379-455; *Dinorben*, 132-4.

84. *Ant. J* XXXIX (1959), 31.

85. *PSAS* XV (1880-1), 326.

86. *PSAS* XVII (1882-3), 90-2.

87. *PSAS* LVIII (1923-4), 11-12 and LXXXIX (1955-6), 181; Leeds, *Celtic Ornament*, 129-30. Fox, *Pattern and Purpose*, 119, dates the comparable belt-plate from York to *c.* 70 A.D. which seems rather too early.

88. *Ant. J* XXXIX (1959), 19-32.

89. *PSAS* XXXVIII (1903-4), 460-5.

90. Unpublished from Hurley Hawkin broch near Dundee, mentioned by permission of D. B. Taylor.

91. Duntulm, Skye, *Ill. London News*, 11.4.1953, now in Nat. Mus. Ants.

92. *P Cambridge AS* XLVII (1953), 30-31. Though from a Belgic grave the Snailwell bracelet (and the Newstead torc) might be ascribed to a South Western workshop because of this decorative technique: cf. *Ant. J* XLI (1961), 195. The nicked wavy line on the edge of the Lochar Moss torc is only an inferior echo.

93. *PSAS* LXVI (1931-2), 301, 369. Childe was mistaken in referring to a spiral armlet. The boss-style rings have a loop on the back and are of different sizes; they cannot be part of a bit (despite *PPS* V (1939), 183);

cf. Stanwick, Yorks., *PPS* XXVIII (1962), 30. Patera dating: Dr R. Nierhaus tells me that from the handle-typology of north European finds the Stanhope patera is not earlier than early second century, more probably mid-second or even early third.

94. J. Anderson, *Scotland in Pagan Times*, I (1883), 135-7. R.C.A.H.M., *Roxburghshire*, 22. *PSAS* XXXVIII (1903-4), 462-6. There is an earlier hinged collar from Dorset, Fox, *Pattern and Purpose*, 107.

95. *J Cork HAS* LXVI (1961), 7-12.

96. *PSAS* LXIX (1934-5), 448-54, add Cairngryffe, Lanarks. (*PSAS* LXXV (1940-1), 217) and Dinas Emrys, Caernarvonshire, 2 (W. F. Grimes, *Prehistory of Wales* (1939), fig. 44).

97. *Problem of the Picts*, ed. Wainwright (1955), 63.

98. L. Alcock, *Dinas Powys* (1963), 69 and 177. The four large jet pin-heads found with the terret from Inverurie, Aberdeenshire (B.M. *Iron Age Guide* (1925), 158) are of a type found in second- and third-century levels at Traprain.

99. *Arch. NL* I, Oct. 1948, 12. R.C.H.M. *York* I (1962), xxxii-iii; Caernarvon and even Caerleon seem to have been destroyed too, *Arch. Camb.* CXI (1962), 110-12, 122-4.

100. *PSAS* LXVI (1931-2), 387-8. *Ant. J* XXXIII (1953), 65-71. *Ant.* XXVII (1953), 219-32. F. T. Wainwright, *The Souterrains of Southern Pictland* (1963).

101. Lecture in Glasgow in 1957; cf. J. Macdonald, *Roman Stones in the Hunterian Museum* (1897), 86-9.

102. *PSAS* LXVI (1931-2), 335, 351, cf. duck brooches with pottery of the later second century at York, R.C.H.M. *York*, I, 91 and pl. 34. A Roman sherd so far defeats dating. The piece of 'typical broch pottery' also from Bow broch corresponds neither in fabric nor in decorative motif to the similarly incised ware found at a few northern broch-sites, and is as likely to be neolithic as iron age. Another supposed connection with northern 'broch-pottery', a vessel from the Antonine Wall fort at Mumrills (*PSAS* LXIII (1928-9), 544-6), has a hard wheel-turned fabric and must have come to Scotland from the south.

103. *PSAS* LXXXV (1950-1). Excavation: 92-117. Glass: 112-13. Quern: 109; its slightly hollow upper surface may perhaps indicate a development from early first-century southern British truncated-cone types, e.g. *Maiden Castle*, 324-9, but its grinding surface is flat.

104. *Roman and Native*, chap. iv.

105. Cramond: *JRS* XLIX (1959), 104 and LII (1962), 163. Carpow: ibid., 163, and *PSAS* XCVI (1962-3), 184-207.

106. *PSAS* LXXXIV (1949-50), Table iii, facing 160; *Aspects of Archaeology*, 204-5. There is a general scarcity in Britain of coins Antoninus to Com-

modus (*Arch. Camb.* CXI (1962), 123), but Scottish hoards ending in Commodus (5) and Severus-Caracalla (4) are sufficiently numerous to make the blank at Traprain seem significant for those times. Despite the continuous series of coins down to Alexander Severus in the hoard at Falkirk buried about 240-50, there is evidence for a decline in the volume of currency in Britain which makes the Traprain gap after Caracalla less cogent: *PSAS* XC (1956-7), 244-6 and LXVIII (1933-4), 35ff.; C. H. V. Sutherland, *Coinage and Currency in Roman Britain* (1937), chap. IV.

107. *PSAS* LXXXIX (1955-6), 288; ibid., 120-2, 143 and 136.

108. Late enamelled dress-fasteners and survivals of animal decoration are all very uncertain (*PSAS* LXXXIX (1955-6), 140 and 180, 135-6). Clarke has instructively pointed out the relative poverty of our Roman imports in the first and second centuries compared with those in eastern Europe further beyond the frontiers (*Roman and Native*, cit. 57-8), and Traprain's third- and fourth-century imports are not supported by many interesting pieces from other places in Scotland.

109. See note 83.

110. This Early and Late division for North Britain was proposed by the writer in *PPS* XXI (1955), 282, but seems more liable to confusion of usage than Pre-Roman Iron Age, Roman Iron Age and Post-Roman Iron Age. The extent of possible confusion is exemplified by the following recent description, 'the "Late" or "Roman" Iron Age of western and northern Scotland, a period which must be taken as commencing only slightly before the first century A.D. and which was culturally exhausted rather before the arrival of the Norse settlers in the late eighth century A.D.' (*Arch. J* CXVIII (1961), 16). It is also surely untenable to restrict 'Britain' to the country south of Forth-Clyde, despite the distinctions we have been considering (*Arch. Camb.* CXI (1962), 4).

111. *PPS* XXI (1955), 291 and *PSAS* XCVII (1963-4), 208-211; *Archaeologia* LXV (1914), 223ff.; *Ant.* XXXIII (1959), 255-7.

112. *Problem of the Picts*, cit. 110-11.

113. S. Piggott, *Neolithic Cultures* (1954), 332.

114. *Prehistory of Scotland*, 181. *PRSE* L (1929-30), 73-4.

Chapter Three

THE SEQUENCE
OF HEBRIDEAN POTTERY

ALISON YOUNG

The archipelago of islands lying off the west coast of Scotland called the Hebrides may be regarded as one unit, but the material under discussion comes mainly from North Uist southwards. That the sea has encroached on the Atlantic coast of the Long Island is shown by the Iron-Age wheel-house structures now half submerged. This is a land of lochs and of peat bogs, a land of extremes, with mile-long stretches of sandy beach, alternating with high cliffs cleft by numberless inlets of the sea.

The wind is a force to be reckoned with, and the sand dunes along the shore, between the sea and the coastal strip, known as the machair, may break in a night and cover acres of cultivated land. Yet, for a pastoral community, the islands offer many advantages. The winters are seldom severe, the sweet grazing of the machair may be changed for high pastures, shelter may be found among the rocky outcrops, and for those with knowledge of wind and tide, many of the islands are accessible one from another almost dryshod.

Evidence of early occupation is not lacking. The pottery kiln-site of Eilean an Tighe,[1] which yielded a remarkable series of Western Neolithic wares, was excavated by Lindsay Scott, who also examined the chambered tombs of Clettraval[2] and Unival,[3] all in North Uist. From these sites, in particular the specialised workshop of Eilean an Tighe, valuable material was recovered, greatly increasing our knowledge of the neolithic in the Hebrides. Both the tombs were reused in the Iron Age; at Clettraval a farm-house and steading were built in the ruins of the burial mound, while at Unival a working-place had distorted the remains of a chambered cairn.

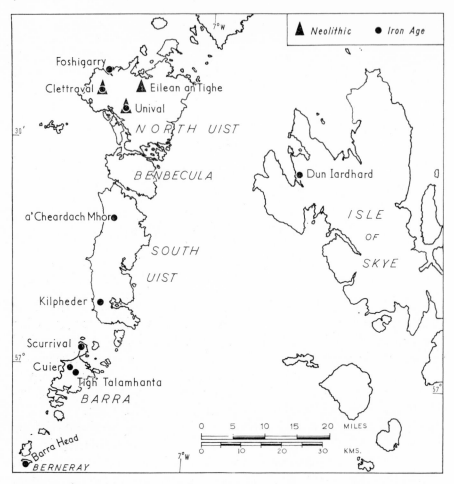

Fig. 1. Sites yielding Neolithic and Iron-Age pottery in Skye and the Outer Hebrides.

The material under discussion was recovered from dwellings of the Iron Age. These consist firstly of aisled-houses, with radial walls or piers, connected with the main walling by two heavy slabs laid horizontally from the top of each pier and bonded into the outer wall, bridging an aisle or space. The divisions so formed were accessible both from the central court and from the back of the bays. Next there are the wheel-houses, where the radial walls form bays unconnected one with another. From the evidence in the Hebrides these structural features appear to have no dating significance. In both cases there is a central court with one or more hearths.

These undefended farm sites are of two types. One type, mainly coastal, is backed against the sand of the machair, with walling too

Pl. 1 *Neolithic pottery from Skara Brae and Rinyo* ($\frac{1}{2}$). (after S. Piggott, *Neolithic Cultures of the British Isles*, 1954, plate VII

*Pl. 2a (above) Neolithic bowl from Unival 1/1; b (below) Hebridean Iron Age pottery:
1, 4, 5, Clettraval; 2, 6–8 Tigh Talamhanta; 3, Dun Iardhard.* (Photo. National
Museum of Antiquities)

inch

slight to have been free standing. Carefully built stone piers support corbelled bays. Such are Kilpheder,[4] an aisled-house, and a' Cheardach Mhor,[5] a wheel-house, both sand-dune or machair sites in South Uist. Kilpheder was apparently deserted at an earlier date than a' Cheardach Mhor, where there is a long pottery sequence of which only the early phase relates to Kilpheder. Comparable sites in North Uist include Foshigarry,[6] Bac mhic Connain[7] and Garry Iochdrach,[8] most of them showing evidence of successive occupation.

The second type of farm-house, which has solid free-standing walling, is typified by Clettraval[9] in North Uist, and Tigh Talamhanta[10] in the Isle of Barra. Both are aisled-houses, built on high plateaux, with good grazing and include new features, a sub-rectangular barn-byre building, and encircling rubble-filled stone wall, useful for stock but of no defensive value. At Tigh Talamhanta the enclosure had a stream running through the farm enceinte, which, in fact, resembles the layout of the steading and in-field of the Scottish Highlands. The pottery from both sites has early and late features, implying a long occupation. The upland farm-house with its stock-yard and barn-byre suggests new methods in farming, introduced perhaps by newcomers seeking more remote homes in troubled times. Arriving possibly without their women-folk, for the pottery forms show no immediate change, these intruders appear to have been absorbed into the existing economy.

These structures are in turn superseded by the defended or galleried-duns, normally built with housing in the stonework of the entrance to take a bar securing the doorway. The duns have an open central court, sometimes with cells or chambers in the thickness of the walls. Though within easy reach of good pasture, these dwellings are built on promontory sites chosen for their defensive value; such are Dun Scurrival and Dun Bahn, each reinforced by walling across the neck of the headland,[11] and the dominant stronghold of Dun Cuier,[12] all three in the Isle of Barra.

From such dwellings comes a sequence of pottery showing strongly marked characteristics, and a second and later, undecorated group which only ends with the Norse invasions.

The pottery from both aisled- and wheel-houses is all ring-built, and, while not conforming to typology or dating accepted for the South, must be classified as Iron Age. The Outer Isles were not directly affected by the Roman occupation of Scotland, and the Iron-Age character of the Hebridean material remains uninfluenced in design and manufacture, with one notable exception, throughout that period, although stray imports have been recorded from the Islands such as the little clay model of a baled fleece[13] from Dun Iardhard in Skye, which suggests some contact with the outer world.

In such a survey of Hebridean Iron-Age pottery it is necessary to consider the background of the Islands, and the pre-Iron-Age material of the Northern Isles.

Professor Piggott has given the earlier picture in his study of the secondary neolithic cultures of north-west Britain.[14] He postulates two intermingling neolithic strains in his Region 2, which includes the Long Island of the Outer Hebrides and the Inner Isles, as well as the northern groups of Orkney and Shetland. While chambered cairns and the kiln site of Eilean an Tighe offer ample proof of neolithic occupation in the Outer Hebrides, the evidence of Bronze Age habitation is slight, and it may be that the Western Isles were little influenced by that culture. It is therefore not unreasonable that some of the decorative elements of the Early Iron-Age Hebridean wares should be found to show evidence of neolithic ancestry.[15]

The patterns on neolithic vessels which can be traced on Iron-Age forms are: incised lattice, herring-bone and chevron, seen on pottery from the Shetland house-site at Ness of Gruting[16] (fig. 2), incised dot or slash-filled ribbon, and applied rondel, illustrated in sherds from Skara Brae and Rinyo in Orkney[17] (pl. 1). The herring-bone pattern can also be seen on wares from Rinyo-Clacton sites[18] as illustrated by a small pot from Creeting St Mary (fig. 3.5). Two associated vessels closely resemble a cup (pl. 2a) found with the latest neolithic burial at Unival which remains so far the only positive ceramic evidence for that culture in the Hebrides.

This ornament may be seen in the earliest group of Iron-Age Hebridean wares which is illustrated in pl. 2b: slashed-filled ribbon and incised dot (no. 1 from Clettraval and no. 2 from Tigh Talamhanta), incised lattice (no. 3 from Dun Iardhard), incised chevron and herring-bone (nos. 4 and 5 from Clettraval) and applied rondel (nos. 7 and 8 from Tigh Talamhanta).

Two purely Iron-Age developments are pin-stamping (pl. 2.6 from Tigh Talamhanta) and finger-channelled decoration (pl. 3.6, from a' Cheardach Mhor).

Incised decoration is found on pots from the earliest levels of the a' Cheardach Mhor wheel-house (pl. 3.1 and 2) these have a weak profile and slightly recurved rim (fig. 4.1 and 3). Vessels with the same rim form, incised decoration and applied fillet were recovered from the Kilpheder aisled-house and appear to be the latest type from that machair site. This early rim is also found at the farm-house of Tigh Talamhanta, on a vessel with distinctive decoration, the impression of a bronze-wire shouldered pin (fig. 4.2). Though the pot is of early form it comes late in the early sequence. This type of decoration was also found on a sherd

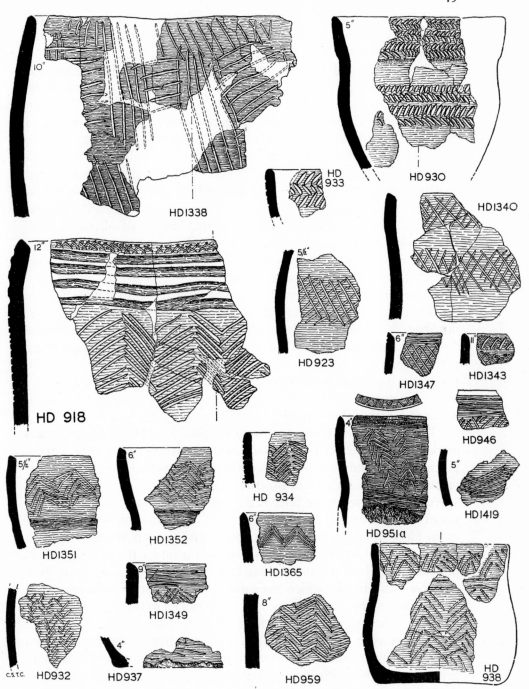

Fig. 2. Neolithic pottery from Ness of Gruting, Shetland. (after *PSAS* LXXXIX, 1955-56, p. 387)

from a midden at a' Cheardach Mhor (pl. 3.8) which demonstrates the overlap between that site and the Tigh Talamhanta aisled-house. The pin-stamping persists and is found on later vessels.[19]

The neolithic sites of Eilean an Tighe and Unival produced charcoals of hazel, oak, pine, willow and birch, but from the Iron-Age levels of the last named site, willow only was recovered. Perhaps a radical alteration in climate and the resultant lack of firewood may represent one factor in the gradual change in pot-making. The baggy vessels, such as those found on the neolithic sites of Clettraval and Unival, may have been replaced by leather bucket forms, though smaller and more easily fired cooking-pots could have kept alive the traditional decorative usage, and indeed, clay vessels would be necessary for cooking. With a developing technique in peat-firing, more especially with the use of adjustable flues to control draught, larger vessels figure on the farmhouse sites, but the earliest Iron-Age sherds decorated with herring-bone, lattice and clay rondels are mainly from smaller pots.

If, however, the Northern Isles, apart from the Unival cup, provide the origins of decoration recurring on pottery in later Hebridean sites, the Western Isles have an Iron-Age characteristic of their own. This is the fillet, applied usually at the greatest girth of the vessel, suggesting perhaps the fictile representation of thonging which would join the two parts of a biconical or situlate leather form—a reasonable shape for a pastoral community (pl. 3.2 and 6 and fig. 4.3-6, from a' Cheardach Mhor and Tigh Talamhanta).

This convention, in its diversity of application, finger-pressed, nail-marked and rilled on in a ribbon pattern, degenerating into a mere pinching up of the clay, is a feature which survives and absorbs intrusive forms with the vigour of an inherited idiom.

A peculiar use of the fillet is its application round the neck of the vessel (pl. 3.3 from a' Cheardach Mhor). This decoration is not confined to the Hebrides and is well represented in Orkney and Shetland.[20] A pot from Lingrow[21] has a slashed cable ornament under the rim, as well as pin-stamping. But the most remarkable of this type is a sherd from Orbister in Shetland[22] which has a thick neck decoration, perhaps representing in clay the thonging, twisted and attached to the neck of a leather bucket, so forming the support for a handle across the top.

Another type of vessel early in the series has an upright rim, not commonly used and not a very practical shape which would tend to break easily. This is illustrated by a large storage jar found in one bay at Tigh Talamhanta (fig. 4.4) among sherds of similar vessels and twig willow charcoals, which suggests the concurrent use of baskets for storage.

These two pot forms, particularly the first, though found in early

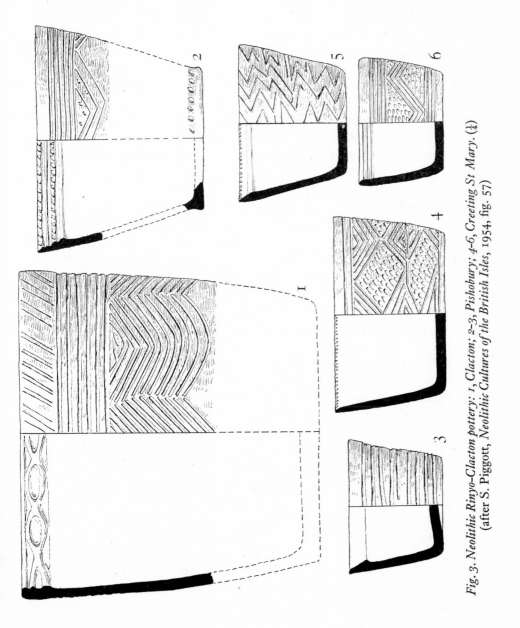

Fig. 3. Neolithic Rinyo–Clacton pottery: 1, Clacton; 2–3, Pishobury; 4–6, Greeting St Mary. (¼)
(after S. Piggott, Neolithic Cultures of the British Isles, 1954, fig. 57)

contexts, have a long life, but they are to some extent superseded by an intrusive type with sharply out-turned rim (fig. 4.5-7, from a' Cheardach Mhor). The characteristic plane of the intrusive rim suggests the copy of a metal prototype, a feature noted by Lindsay Scott in describing his Type 1a pottery from Clettraval.[23] There may have been an earlier contact with Rome in the North, as recorded by Bede,[24] but typical bronze 'kettles' (pl. 4a) such as were found at Newstead (A.D. 78–189) indicate a possible source for the new form, deriving ultimately from Agricola's campaign, when that imaginative leader used the fleet in support of land forces in his invasion of Scotland. Tacitus notes that the fleet of Agricola 'discovered and subdued the Orkney Islands hitherto unknown'[25] at a date generally accepted as A.D. 83 or 84. Stories in Holinshed's Chronicles do not throw such a rosy light on the invasion as does Tacitus, Agricola's son-in-law and biographer. The later account indicates that natives, employed by the Romans to pilot the fleet through the narrows and tide races of the Northern Isles, unmindful of their own lives, deliberately wrecked the invading ships. While this is an unconfirmed tale, it is more than probable that there must have been wrecks in the treacherous seaways of the North, and an island people would be perfectly competent to deal faithfully with such disasters and doubtless profited thereby.

As may be seen from the upper division of the table, fig. 5, a study of the material shows a wide distribution of the form. Not only in the Orkneys can this intrusive rim be traced. At Jarlshof[26] in Shetland, Mr Hamilton's Class II pottery from aisled-house and wheel-house levels, includes a swelling shoulder with everted rim closely comparable to examples from a' Cheardach Mhor in the Hebrides. From both sites there are sherds which show fluting on the inner surface of the rim (fig. 4.5, from a' Cheardach Mhor), a feature seen on pottery from other sites in the Shetlands, as well as in Orkney.[27] Mr Hamilton, in describing the Jarlshof vessels, observes that this ware reflects the intrusion of new ceramic traditions.

With the advent of the everted rim, incised wares go out of fashion. An arcaded, finger-channelled ornament is, however, found on the upper part of vessels, a characteristic peculiar to the Hebrides, and illustrated on sherds from a' Cheardach Mhor (fig. 4.5 and 6 and pl. 3.6).[28]

From the last site were recovered the bases of pots in this series decorated on the inside with thumb-prints and wide shallow grooves (pl. 3.4, 7 and 9).

The older forms persist, however, as does the applied decoration, now also transferred to the vessels with everted rim, typifying the absorption of new styles in a traditional pottery craft. The native conven-

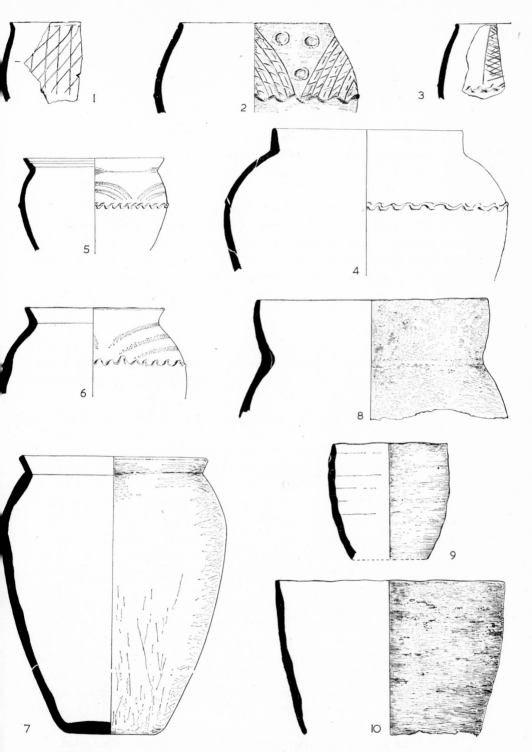

Fig. 4. Hebridean Iron-Age pottery-types: 1, 3, 5-7, a' Cheardach Mhor; 2 and 4, Tigh Talamhanta; 8-10, Dun Cuier. ($\frac{1}{4}$)

tions are applied on the intrusive form with its sharply bevelled rim and more shapely profile.

The pottery of the next phases, though Iron-Age in character, must be classified by the associated material as Dark-Age.

A reconstructed pot (pl. 4b) from an intrusive shelter dug into one of the bays of the ruined wheel-house at a' Cheardach Mhor (Phase II) has irregular decoration of the girth strip, a feature paralleled by sherds from dun sites, such as Scurrival and Cuier[29] in the Isle of Barra, suggesting a late date. This may, like another innovation, the flaring rim (fig. 4.8, from Dun Cuier), be associated with the duns.

At Dun Cuier, some of these long rimmed vessels show applied decoration at the neck,[30] but the majority were plain. Rims of this form also figure in high levels at Clettraval[31] and the Iron-Age working-place at Unival.[32] They have not been found associated with aisled-houses or wheel-houses in primary levels, but coincide apparently with the change in dwelling plan, from the radial stone settings of the farm-houses to the open court of the duns.

The last variant of the Hebridean sequence is a type of plain pottery which may be identified with the pre-Norse phase (fig. 4.9 and 10, from Dun Cuier). The form has a weak profile, the rim often pressed on with the finger-tips, though straight-sided vessels are also found. The paste of this poorly made type is uneven and brittle, and the surface harsh. Neither potting nor firing are highly skilled. The exterior is usually sooty. No decoration, so constant a feature of the earlier wares, is present. This is a definite break with the tradition of ornamented pottery.

While commonly found in duns, this ware occurs sporadically in the upper levels of the wheel-house sites. At a' Cheardach Mhor, sherds of the fabric were found in high-level middens, related to poorly built curved walling, set in the sandy mound which formed over the wheel-house.[33]

It has been suggested elsewhere that this rather formless cooking-ware has affinities with Northern Irish sites, and possibly follows on contacts with Dalriada which may well have originated in the preceding stage.[34] At Dun Cuier many sherds of the type were found in a cooking-hearth, as though left in the peat-ash on breaking and merely replaced.

This is the typical pottery of the last occupants of the duns and may be linked to the penetration of Scotic raiders, who, primarily settling in Argyll, are known to have invaded the Isles. The main Dalriadan settlement is dated to the sixth century A.D.

The Hebridean Iron-Age sequence shows, firstly, forms with a weak rim and profile, decorated with incised patterns, in some cases bearing the

Pl. 3 *Iron-Age pottery from a' Cheardach Mhor, South Uist.*

inches

Pl. 4a Roman kettle from Newstead.(Photo. National Museum of Antiquities)

inches

Pl. 4b Iron-Age pot, a' Cheardach Mhor, South Uist.

	Inner Isles	Outer Isles	Orkney	Shetland	Caithness	Sutherland
Everted Rim	Dun Beag	a' Cheardach Mhor Bev. Coll. N.M.A. Clettraval Foshigarry Gherisclett Tigh Talamhanta	Ayre broch Cairston Midhowe Okstrow	Jarlshof Mousa broch Sae Breck	Keiss broch Road broch	Kintradwell
Inner Rim Fluting	Dun Beag	a' Cheardach Mhor Foshigarry	Ayre broch Cairston Midhowe Okstrow	Clumlie Cumlins Jarlshof Mousa broch Sae Breck		
Applied Decoration	Dun Beag Dun Iardhard Dun Nighean	North Uist Benbecula South Uist Barra	Ayre broch Burrian Lingrow Scapa		Everley broch Road broch Skirza broch	
Fingerchannelled	Dun Beag	a' Cheardach Mhor Clettraval Tigh Talamhanta				
Decorated Base	Dun Beag	a' Cheardach Mhor Bev. Coll. N.M.A.	Lingrow West Howe	Burra broch Cumlins Gletness Sae Breck	Keiss broch Nybster Road broch White broch	

Fig. 5. Table showing distribution of pottery types.

impress of a bronze-wire shouldered pin. These were possibly used concurrently with leather vessels, from which the applied stitched convention is derived. While no close dating is offered for this initial phase, Mrs Fowler's argument for the updating of the Scottish Iron Age[35] would allow for an earlier appearance of this type of pin than the first/second-century dating formerly postulated.[36]

A first/second century A.D. date is suggested for the beginning of the next phase by the appearance of yellow vitreous beads[37] found in the machair wheel-house of a' Cheardach Mhor and the upland farm-house of Tigh Talamhanta. Allowing for the transmutation of a metal form into the ceramic sequence, this stage coincides with the appearance of a vessel with a more decided profile and sharply everted rim, a type common to the northern mainland of Scotland and the Northern Isles, but in the Hebrides distinguished by the characteristic girth decoration, in some instances associated with a fluted inner rim and arcaded ornament. This form has a long life and includes larger and sometimes plain pots. From this time onwards pottery with incised decoration would appear to be no longer in fashion in the Hebrides. The pin-stamped sherds, the yellow vitreous beads and the sharply everted rim forms reflect contact with the Scottish mainland.

The following phases equate with the irregular decoration of the earlier dun wares, while the last corresponds in time with the poorly made plain pottery from the duns, dwellings built for strength on defensive sites. Resulting perhaps from Irish contacts, this may be dated from A.D. 500 or a little earlier.[38]

The break in the Hebridean tradition of incised wares would denote the absorption of new pottery styles by a self-sufficient pastoral people, concerned merely with survival, content to farm and fish, making little progress in material equipment; while the coarse dun wares suggest the intrusion of colonists pressed on by land hunger, entrenching themselves in unknown country. For the Hebrideans, shelter and grazing were paramount, for the newcomers, defence.

Postscript

Since this paper was written in 1961, Mr Euan MacKie has excavated at Dun Mor Vaul.[39] His 'pre-broch midden' pottery, phase 1, includes barrel-shaped vessels not hitherto noted on Hebridean sites (fig. 1.1-3), but in the same group are included pots with S-shaped profile and incised decoration (fig. 1.4, 10, 11) which show some affinity with sherds from the earliest phase at a' Cheardach Mhor (fig. 5.1 and 2) and pottery with decoration clearly related to wheel-house wares. The full report on the Dun Mor Vaul excavations is awaited with interest.

Notes

1. Scott, W. L., *PSAS* LXXXV (1950-1), 1.
2. Scott, W. L., *PPS* XIV (1948), 46.
3. Scott, W. L., *PSAS* LXXXII (1947-8), 1.
4. Lethbridge, T. C., *PPS* XVIII (1952), 176.
5. Young, Alison and Richardson, K. M., *PSAS* XCIII (1959-60), 135.
6. Callander, J. G., *PSAS* LXV (1930-1), 299.

7. Callander, J. G., *PSAS* LXVI (1931-2), 42.

8. Beveridge, Erskine, *PSAS* LXVI (1931-2), 32.

9. Scott, W. L., *PPS* XIV (1948), 46.

10. Young, Alison, *PSAS* LXXXVII (1952-3), 80.

11. Young, Alison, *PSAS* LXXXIX (1955-6), 290, pl. XXII.3 and 4.

12. Ibid., pl. XXIII.

13. Macleod, F. T., *PSAS* XLIX (1914-15), 57, fig. 11.

14. Piggott, Stuart, *The Neolithic Cultures of the British Isles* (1954), 321.

15. A similar, though later, fossilisation of type occurs in the Hebrides, where hand-mills, little differing from the rotary querns of the Iron Age (e.g. from Cuier in Barra, *PSAS* LXXXIX (1955-6), 290, pl. XXII.2) were shown by E. C. Curwen to be commonly used in the Islands in 1937 (*Ant.* XI (1937), 148)—a greater discrepancy in time, allowing for the quern type to be dated third-fourth century A.D., than the 1,500 years suggested for the survival of ornament on Western Neolithic pottery.

16. Henshall, A. S., *PSAS* LXXXIX (1955-6), 381.

17. Piggott, Stuart, op. cit., 321, and pl. XII.

18. Ibid., fig. 57.

19. Young, Alison, *PSAS* LXXXVII (1952-3), 84, pl. IX.4, sherd from Eye Peninsula, Lewis, impressed by a pin with a movable ring-head, a development of the shouldered pin, and dated by R. B. K. Stevenson to eighth/ninth century A.D.; see also Stevenson, R. B. K., *PPS* XXI (1955), 292.

20. Hamilton, J. R. C., *Excavations at Jarlshof, Shetland*, H.M.S.O. 1956, figs. 25 and 26.

21. Young, Alison, *PSAS* LXXXVII (1952-3), 80, pl. IX.2.

22. Nat. Mus. Ants., Edinburgh, unpublished.

23. *PPS* XIV (1948), 61.

24. Bede, *Hist. Eccles.* I; 3.

25. *Agricola* X; 5.

26. Hamilton, J. R. C., *Jarlshof* (see note 20), p. 64, fig. 35.

27. Ibid., fig. 35.3 and p. 65, comparative material.

28. See also sherds from Clettraval, Scott, W. L., *PPS* XIV (1948), 46, pl. VIII, and Tigh Talamhanta, Young, Alison, *PSAS* LXXXVII (1952-3), 80, fig. 8.86.

29. Young, Alison, *PSAS* LXXXIX (1955-6), 290, fig. 2.3 and fig. 12.104, 105.

30. Ibid., fig. 9.50 and 57.

31. Scott, W. L., *PPS* XIV (1948), 46, fig. 6, VI3, on right.

32. Scott, W. L., *PSAS* LXXXII (1947-8), I, fig. 3, A6.

33. Young, Alison and Richardson, K. M., *PSAS* XCIII (1959-60), 151, fig. 10.45-57.

34. Young, Alison, *PSAS* LXXXIX (1955-6), 301 and 311.

35. Fowler, Elizabeth, *PPS* XXVI (1960), 161-4.

36. Young, Alison, *PSAS* LXXXVII (1952-3), 92 and Burley, E., *PSAS* LXXXIX (1955-6), 167, nos. 96, 97.

37. Mrs C. M. Piggott considered these beads characteristic of the first/second century A.D. in these islands, *PSAS* LXXXVII (1952-3), 104, Appendix A.

38. In his 'Consular Chronology of Dark Age Britain', Mr P. K. Johnstone quotes a traditional dating of A.D. 464 for the arrival of the Scots in Argyll, *Ant.* XXXVI (1962), 108.

39. *Ant.* XXXIX (1965), 268.

Chapter Four

THE HILL-FORTS
OF NORTHERN BRITAIN

R. W. FEACHEM

The hill-forts and large settlements are distributed in varying degrees of density throughout all the Provinces of Northern Britain, but none occur in Orkney and Shetland. Measured from north to south, from Dunnet Head to Darlington, the territory is about 300 miles in length, a similar figure to that of the comparable measure over Southern Britain; but the area of the north part is only about half that of the south, and of this only a restricted proportion was land fit for settlement. The present nature of the vegetation throughout the region (see map at end) must reflect the general picture prevailing in the last part of the first millennium B.C.;[1] for although the improvements of the last two centuries have brought about a few such spectacular reforms as the draining of the upper part of the Forth valley and the enrichment of Strathmore, as well as a general betterment of good ground, they have had little effect on the ratio between the richer and the poorer soils. The land over 2,000 feet—in darker grey on the map—supports only Arctic-Alpine vegetation and Sub-Alpine Moors, and the hatched areas represent the Peat Moors, Mosses and Bogs, the Wet 'Grass' Moors, and the Acid Grasslands. In contrast, the unhatched remainder of the land represents the better areas, described as 'Dry' Grass Moors, Heather Moors, and what is now Improved Land. This includes the extensive 'Dry' Grass Moors drained by the River Tweed and its tributaries, and the Heather Moors which dominate some 3,000 square miles of the north-east region of the Grampian Mountains, as well as the richer soils in the east and throughout the Midland Valley.

In Northern Britain, most of the settlements of the third, second and early first millennia B.C. still elude discovery; and the earliest domestic sites so far on record are the unenclosed platform settlements,[2] some of which comprise up to a dozen houses and must have sheltered considerable numbers of people. The absence of any form of enclosing fence, wall or rampart seems to deny them an Iron Age cultural background, even though they may have been built and occupied in the third quarter of the first millennium B.C. It will suffice here, therefore, merely to recall their existence before considering the enclosed settlements.

At present, the remains of some 1,500 hill-forts and large settlements of all kinds have been recorded in Northern Britain, the majority having been visited within the last fifteen years. This comprehensive programme of field survey has not yet been matched by an equally vigorous and illuminating campaign of competent excavations; unless and until the results of even the earlier stages of such an operation become available, evidence for the dating of the great majority of the hill-forts and large settlements must remain a matter of enlightened speculation. A distribution map of these remains alone can, as yet, indicate little more than their accumulation over at least half a millennium, which is of comparatively small significance, as the spread is adequately shown by the distribution of the better land. In conjunction with the known distribution of other types of settlements, however, that of hill-forts and large settlements does assume a certain importance, which is illustrated and discussed below.

The remains of the hill-forts and large settlements of Northern Britain—the communal rather than the individual dwelling-places—include examples dating from different times within the period concerned, serving various purposes, differing in size and constructed in a variety of techniques. They represent colonisation and expansion, and they show evidence of the evolution of political cohesion; for their growth and multiplication accompanied the transformation from the amorphous, semi-nomadic pastoral life which seems to have been general up to the beginning of the period, to the development of some at least partly organised societies, fit to be named and, in some cases, treated with by the Romans. In some areas the presence of only a thin scatter of remains challenges explanation, in others heavy concentrations imply enduring activity and prosperity. Above all, the surveys have shown that regional types can be recognised from surface indications; and that the surface remains of enough multi-period hill-forts and settlements remain in a good enough state of preservation to allow a considerable amount of important information about structural sequences to be gleaned from plans alone, without excavation. The Provinces and Regions of Northern

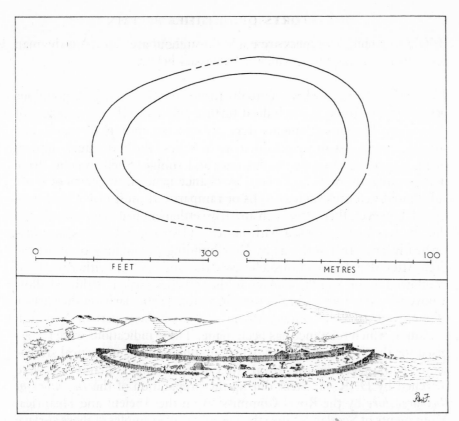

Fig. 1. White Hill, Peeblesshire.　　　Fig. 2. (below) Hayhope Knowe, Roxburghshire.

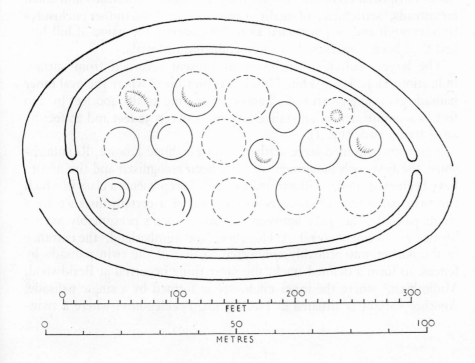

Britain to which references are made throughout are shown on the map reproduced in chapter 1, which is discussed below.

Timber Structures. In what eventually turned out to be the more populous parts of the country, if not indeed further afield as well, the defences of the earliest known settlements were constructed entirely of wood. The palisades were usually embedded in trenches, the individual timbers being chocked and packed with stones and rubble. Such trenches have not infrequently been discovered by chance beneath the ruins of more substantial defences such as walls or ramparts. It must often have happened, however, that, after such an early settlement had been abandoned, the site was neither reused with newer and stronger defences, nor disturbed in any other way—as by later buildings, ploughing or afforestation. After abandonment in such cases, the timbers were either removed or allowed to rot, and the packing in the trenches settled. A thin, shallow groove was thus formed in the topsoil, visible particularly on the surface of the extensive 'Dry' Grass Moors in the southern part of Northern Britain to which reference has been made. These indications were recognised for the first time in 1946, when air-photographs in vertical stereoscopic pairs, taken by the Royal Air Force, became available and were searched by Dr K. A. Steer during the preparation of the *Inventory of Roxburghshire* by the Royal Commission on the Ancient and Historical Monuments of Scotland. Since then numbers of examples of these surface traces have been recorded, among them *einzelhof* homesteads and small farmsteads,[3] settlements of medium and large size, and timber enclosures large enough and so positioned as to have earned the name of hill-fort had they been constructed of more enduring materials.

The largest palisaded enclosure at present recorded from surface indications alone is on White Hill, in Peeblesshire,[4] where the oval inner palisade enclosing an area of $1\frac{3}{4}$ acres, measuring axially 400 feet by 240 feet, is accompanied at a distance varying between 50 feet and 20 feet by an outer palisade (fig. 1).

The twin-palisaded large settlement at Hayhope Knowe, Roxburghshire, the first such monument to have been recognised and the first to have been excavated,[5] is illustrated in fig. 2. It represents a class in which the twin-palisaded enclosure is surrounded at a certain distance by a single palisade, the space between the two elements presumably having formed a convenient corral. At Huckhoe, Northumberland,[6] the entrance in the outlier was probably connected to that of the twin palisade by fences, to form a defined track; the same thing occurred at Braidwood, Midlothian,[7] where the inner enclosure is formed by a single palisade. Another variant is situated at Horsburgh, Peeblesshire, where a twin-palisaded enclosure one acre in extent is surrounded at a distance varying between 40 feet and 20 feet by an outer twin palisade the elements of which lie 15 feet apart (fig. 3).

It is virtually certain that the all-timber hill-forts and large settlements were the earliest defended communal enclosures, at least in the

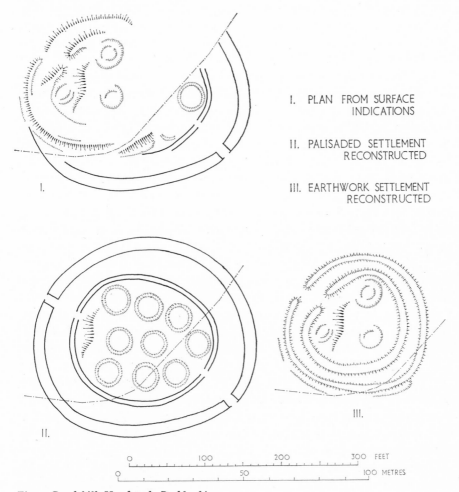

I. PLAN FROM SURFACE
         INDICATIONS

II. PALISADED SETTLEMENT
          RECONSTRUCTED

III. EARTHWORK SETTLEMENT
          RECONSTRUCTED

Fig. 3. Castlehill, Horsburgh, Peeblesshire.

southern part of Northern Britain. The most northerly example yet confirmed underlies the visible remains of the promontory fort at Inchtuthil, Perthshire,[8] and the westernmost crowns a low hill at Glenehervie, five miles south of Campbeltown, Argyll. The part of the country thus defined accounts for more than 90 per cent of the recorded hill-forts and large settlements. As has been remarked above, the precise dating of the great majority of all-timber settlements is at present uncertain; and at

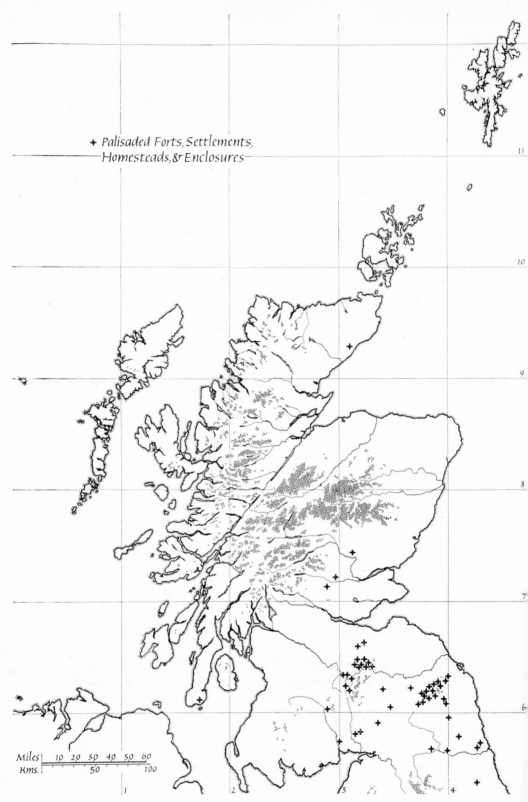

+ Palisaded Forts, Settlements, Homesteads, & Enclosures

Miles 10 20 30 40 50 60
Kms. 50 100

Fig. 4. Palisaded Forts, Settlements, Homesteads and Enclosures.

the same time their number and distribution is unknown and unknowable, in that so many underlie later defences, or have been otherwise obliterated. Allowing for these and other handicaps, and taking into consideration such places as Staple Howe[9] and the now quite large number of first-period all-timber defences which have been unearthed from beneath the later defences of hill-forts, it can be suggested that the earliest may represent the settlements of expanding communities of possibly the fourth and probably the third century B.C. The expansion referred to would have been from the smaller settlements and the homesteads. The distribution of all the palisaded works so far recorded in the region, shown in fig. 4, includes the smaller units as well as the larger ones. The single outlier, in Caithness, is a homestead recorded by Mr J. L. Davidson of the Archaeology Division, Ordnance Survey. Apart from a possible example near Nairn, this is the only one of its kind now known north of the Forth. Since no intensive search has yet been made in the North-Eastern Province, it can only be surmised that there, as elsewhere, all-timber dwellings and enclosures were used by the earlier Iron Age inhabitants.

An alternative method of mounting palisades, which has recently been recorded at Harehope and at Woolshears Wood, in Peeblesshire,[10] had the effect of freeing settlers from the technical difficulties and hard labour inherent in digging a steep-sided, narrow trench, often in more or less solid rock. This entailed making a comparatively low bank and sinking the palisade trench along its crest. At Harehope there are two banks, the material for which was dug out of a broad, shallow medial ditch; at Woolshears Wood, one. Settlements, and even hill-forts, defended by low, almost insignificant banks unworthy of the name rampart, are widespread throughout the region. Although no other examples have been tested, it is at least possible that the embanked palisade, as it is called, eventually came into general use, and superseded the original kind. Whether it was ancestral to the rows of large stakes planted at intervals in true ramparts, as at Bonchester Hill,[11] must at present remain uncertain.

Timber-Laced Walls. All-timber hill-forts and large settlements are widespread throughout the greater part of the better land in Northern Britain. Also widely spread are hill-forts some part or the whole of whose defences consist of walls which are known to have incorporated a timber lacing in one form or another. Where these have been destroyed by fire, with resulting vitrifaction, such works are not difficult to identify. The unknown number of examples, however, which were not burned, and so exhibit no vitrifaction, is probably large. As at present known, the spread of such structures in Northern Britain starts well up in the little narrow strips of usable land in the north west, and ends at Edgerston, in Roxburghshire; but there is no reason why other examples should not occur elsewhere. The great variety of size and shape exhibited among the seventy-eight examples now on record, coupled with the differences in structural detail which are evident even in the fragmentary and minute amount of solid information that has so far been acquired about them, underlines the commonplace fact that the mere occurrence of a timber-laced wall is in itself of little significance in the elucidation of any of the general problems posed by hill-forts and large settlements, or in dating them. It will suffice here to recall that at Burghead, in Moray, there exist the mutilated remains of the only example yet discovered in Great Britain of a nailed timber framework. Mrs M. A. Cotton[12] has described it as of 'Avaricum Type'; but, noting the absence of knowledge of the associated cultural material, and of other structural details, has concluded that any attempt to assign a date to the work must at present be all speculation.

Apart from this, only two points call for remark here. The first concerns what Childe called the Abernethy forts, basing his isolation of such a group on the known occurrence of the orifices or beam-holes (that once held transverse timbers) on either the outer or the inner or both faces of the wall. Knowledge of such occurrences, as it must of necessity still be, depended upon random chance; and it was impossible then as it still is now to form any useful idea about how many hill-forts with this characteristic there may be—and indeed, to what extent the feature concerned is really distinctive. The six forts originally selected as representatives of the class included four about which excavation reports, assumed to be reliable at least in regard to the main details, were available: Abernethy itself, Forgandenny, Monifieth and Finavon, the last excavated by Childe. In addition to these, Castle Law, Midlothian, and Dun More, Perthshire, were included. It now transpires that the latter was included in error; while recent excavations[13] have demonstrated that the timber-and-stone element at Castle Law represents nothing but the foundation of a gatehouse, and that beyond its limit the rampart is wholly composed of white clay.

A glance at the simplified plan in fig. 5 exposes striking disparities between the plans of the four remaining original 'Abernethy' forts. Abernethy is a small and roundly oval contour fort, univallate save for a horn-work; Forgandenny is a little larger but is bivallate, and is pierced by a line of walling such as has been recorded elsewhere only at Knock Farril, Ross-shire, and in the 'out-fort', now destroyed, adjacent to Barry Hill, Alyth, Perthshire. Monifieth is large and somewhat piriform, with arcs of outer

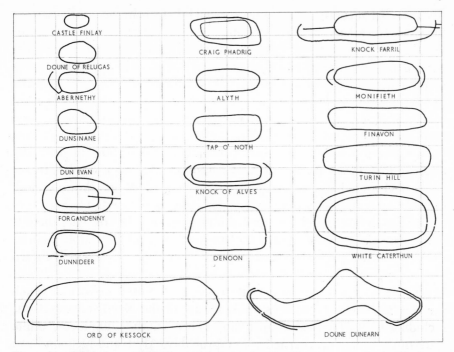

Fig. 5. Simplified plans of Hill-Forts with timber-laced walls or ramparts in the North-eastern province (squares of 100 feet, 30·5 metres).

walling covering either end; and Finavon is a decidedly flat-sided oblong univallate work. Although the real significance of structural similarities is hard to assess, it is unlikely that a systematist would have selected these four as belonging to a class merely from looking at their plans. At the same time, no information is available about the presence or absence of the orifices of beam-holes in any other of the forts shown in fig. 5.

As far as relics are concerned, the situation at present is simply that a few articles have been recorded as coming from a few forts; and the information which can be extracted from them must be used, in consequence, with very great reserve.

The net result of consideration of all available evidence was perhaps best summed up by Mrs Cotton,[14] even though the various dates then suggested can now be modified. There is indeed little enough to generalise about; but before leaving the subject to consider the appearance and significance of the recognisable regional classes of hill-forts and large settlements—among which certain timber-laced types occur—it may be useful to make the second particular observation referred to above, which concerns the oblong forts such as Finavon. The distinction between a contour fort and a structure built to a preconceived plan is difficult to draw if the shape of the chosen site is very regular. Nevertheless, the suggestion that certain of the timber-laced hill-forts in the North-Eastern Province were laid out in the form of a rather narrow oblong may be justified, whatever its significance may be. In fig. 5, for example, the general appearance of the oblong with its longer sides drawn straight is marked in the plans of Forgandenny and Dunnideer, in those comprising the five examples in the central column which include the problematical Knock of Alves, and in those of Knock Farril, Finavon and the uncertain Turin Hill in the right-hand column.[15] All these are built on hills which allow space for such a plan, but in no case is this made obligatory by restriction imposed by the lie of the ground. The same applies in the cases of Monifieth and the White Caterthun, even though these are both a good deal less rigidly oblong, and the latter is not certainly known to be timber-laced, though the probability is strong. In contrast, the five little vitrified forts at the top of the left-hand column are simply contour forts, as indeed are the much elongated Ord of Kessock and Dunearn forts.

It may be noted that large cisterns, excavated into the rock of which the sites are formed, can be seen in several of the North-Eastern forts, including Craig Phadrig, Dun Evan, Tap o' Noth, Dunnideer, White Caterthun, Finavon, Abernethy and, probably, Alyth and Denoon Law. The presence of close outworks is also of interest. All the forts except probably Tap o' Noth have them, ranging from a mere arc covering an approachable flank to a complete encirclement. As a rule the outer work is less substantial than the inner, though it may nevertheless have formed a serious obstacle. While little is known about the true character of most of the outer defences, the example at Craig Phadrig can be seen to be vitrified. There is no evidence to show whether this is contemporary with the inner defence—itself a typical oblong vitrified fort with a cistern— or whether the latter represents a re-use of the site as has been observed, for example, at Benderloch, in Argyll.[16]

These and other problems which spring to mind simply cannot be answered in the meagre glimmerings of existing evidence; but it may at least be borne in mind that a class of hill-fort identified by a peculiarity of plan and, possibly, by the presence of a rock-hewn cistern, does seem to exist in the North-Eastern Province, and that an iron ring-headed pin possibly assignable to the third century B.C. was found in one probable member (Monifieth).[17]

Unfinished Structures. There is however a point of contact between one fort of this supposed class and one belonging to quite a different group. This group comprises seven unfinished forts, all comparatively large, which are situated in the North-Eastern Province. The one referred to

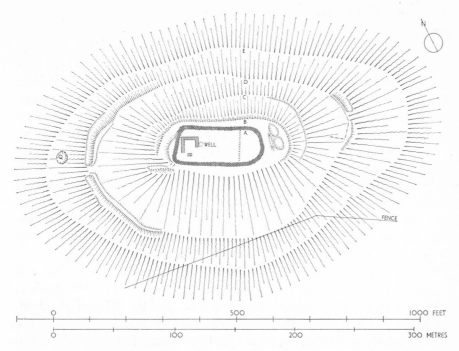

Fig. 6. Dunnideer, Aberdeenshire.

occupies the Hill of Dunnideer, in Aberdeenshire (fig. 6). The outermost
unfinished line of defence (E) is represented only by a slight terrace, the
remains of a marker-trench, situated well down the flanks of the hill and
enclosing an area measuring axially 950 feet by 600 feet. Gaps for entrances have been left at either apex. Next, a line D, similarly marked out,
lies between 50 feet and 150 feet inside line E. In this case work on the
construction of a rampart has begun on either side of each entrance-gap.
The third line (C), which cannot be followed across the steep south-west
flank of the hill, is otherwise similar to the outer pair. The fourth line (B)
is a ruinous stony bank, feeble at best and absent on the steep south-
west flank. The innermost defence (A) is the heavily-vitrified wall of the
oblong fort already mentioned, which contains a contemporary cistern
and a mediaeval tower. These remains represent those of a complete but
vitrified oblong fort, probably with an outwork (B), and those of an incomplete trivallate system of defence. The choice of two interpretations
is clear: on the one hand it could be supposed that the oblong fort was
built on a hill already furrowed with abandoned, incomplete defences—
these having been abandoned either as a result of the arrival of the
builders of the now vitrified fort or at an earlier date; on the other hand,
it could be supposed that the unfinished multivallate work (together with

the others of the group), being of a sophisticated design embodying the principle of defence in depth, was part of a hasty scheme of resistance to an enemy who, in the event, either forbade their completion in the light of his victory or rendered it unnecessary in view of his defeat. Multivallate defences have been shown to be late pre-Roman features in Northern Britain, as elsewhere, and there is no reason why these should be exceptional. While there is justification for suggesting that the timber-laced fort may have been constructed at an earlier date than that, there is no reason why occupation should not have continued into the last quarter of the first century A.D.

Six of the seven unfinished forts referred to, of which Dunnideer is one, lie in the eighty miles between central Strathmore and Spey Bay, in territory where hill-forts are scarce though the land is good. They include the unfinished hill-fort at Kinpurney Hill, Angus, which with an area of 16½ acres is by far the largest north of the Forth. This one, and examples at Knockargetty Wood, Aberdeenshire, and on Durn Hill and Little Conval, in Banffshire, occupy new sites. The Dunnideer circumstances are paralleled at the remaining example, the White Caterthun, in Angus. It is possible that this great stone-walled fort (presumably timber-laced) and the smaller stronghold at Dunnideer were selected to be further defended for the emergency by the potentates residing in them, or ruling from them, and that other local rulers decided that defences were now required in places far from existing hill-forts—as are the Banffshire sites and Knockargetty Wood. Whatever may be the truth, and however fragmentary the story may be, it is difficult not to equate the emergency with the advance of the Romans from Strathmore to the Spey; and the defeat at Mons Graupius for the abandonment of the works, which thereafter remained as memorials to a policy of 'too little and too late'.

Space forbids detailed accounts of the unfinished forts, from which a considerable amount of information on constructional methods can be extracted.

Regional Types. These brief reviews of the all-timber hill-forts and large settlements and of some of those with timber-laced walls or ramparts, together with the incident of the unfinished structures in the North-Eastern Province, can now be followed by summaries of some of the identifiable regional groups, starting in the northern part of the country in Regions 47 and 48 of the Atlantic Province, the territories of the Cornovii, the Smertae and the Lugi. Each one of the few hill-forts known in this area is formed by a single stone wall defending a hill-top, such as Buaile Oscar (fig. 7), at Dorrery. The striking peculiarity shared by these

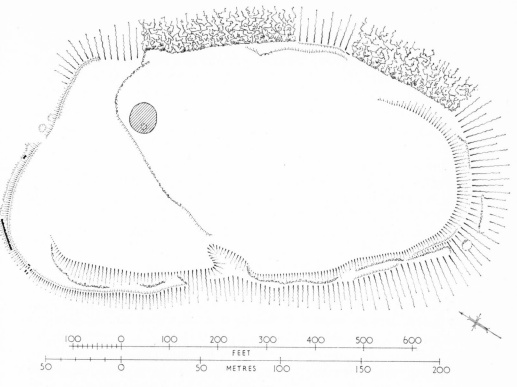

Fig. 7. Buaile Oscar, Beinn Freiceadain, Caithness.

forts, and still well preserved not only at the example illustrated but in particular at Garrywhin, Caithness, and Duchary Rock, Sutherland, is the lining of the gateways with massive stone slabs, which is not recorded elsewhere. It is a local translation into stone of the wooden sheathing of the rampart terminals, presumably brought about here by the availability of suitable slabs of sedimentary rock. In cases where the fabric of the adjacent stretches of the wall is considerably wasted, the slabs remaining erect are grouped in a manner which, at first sight, suggests the sidewalls of a large denuded cist. Nothing is known of the date of these works.

The dominant type among the hill-forts of Region 44 is the small stone-walled structure which may often, though not always, exhibit vitrifaction. Examples are Castle Finlay, the Doune of Relugas and Dun Evan, simplified plans of which are shown in fig. 5. The northernmost, Dun Creich, is situated on the shore of the Dornoch Firth; none is known east of the Spey; but they occur, often very small in size, along the shores of Loch Ness and as far down the Great Glen as Auchteraw, on the River Oich. At present but little is known about the hill-forts of Lochaber, Lorn and Northern Argyll, and it is too early to form an

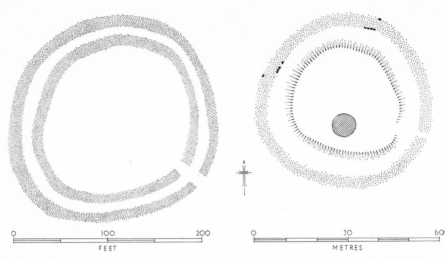

Fig. 8. Left, Cairnmore, Aberdeenshire; right, The Barmkyn of North Keig, Aberdeenshire.

opinion on the question whether such structures can be said to have spread up from the west coast, as may seem very probable. Again, nothing is known about the date of these structures.

In Region 41, modern Aberdeenshire excluding Buchan (Region 43), about half the known hill-forts are of a distinct local type—stone-walled structures such as Cairnmore and the Barmkyn of North Keig (fig. 8)—which have one or two heavy ruinous walls and are almost circular on plan. Two examples of these lie within what are almost certainly earlier structures, one on Barra Hill, Old Meldrum, and the other at Echt (fig. 9). Here the triple ramparts have as many as five entrances, but the stone walls within them only use two—numbered 2 and 4 on the plan—while hollow ways associated with entrances 1, 3 and 5 can be seen to protrude into the interior as formed by the inner stone wall. At Barra Hill the ratio of entrances is 3 to 1. The multiplicity of entrances at Echt and Barra Hill is uncommon; but the Brown Caterthun, in Region 40, exhibits the same phenomenon carried to an extreme (fig. 10). This assemblage of concentric ruins crowns a low hill the summit of which, at 943 feet above sea-level, is located near the entrance of the innermost feature, a very ruinous wall enclosing an area measuring axially only 300 feet by 200 feet. This lies within a five-acre enclosure formed by a ruined wall accompanied by a double rampart. These three lines of defence have as many as nine entrances. This circumstance must prompt enquiry into whether the gaps are in fact all entrances or whether they might represent unlinked sections of a defence started by gangs but not completed. On the ground the precision with which they all end is impressive,

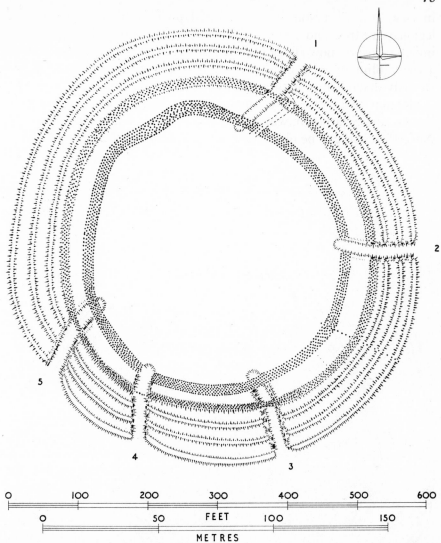

Fig. 9. The Barmekin of Echt, Aberdeenshire.

apparently exhibiting a greater degree of neatness than might be sup-posed to have resulted from the unfinished work of gangs. These works are in turn enclosed first by a bank and then by a rampart with an external quarry-ditch, both the latter being pierced by eight entrances. Nothing is known about the dates of the forts in these Regions.

In Region 39—Strathtay—eight out of the seventeen recorded hill-forts are multivallate works the innermost defences of which take the form of a walled enclosure and the outer of ramparts—the latter in almost all cases eked out with natural rock-faces and precipices. The King's Seat at Dunkeld (fig. 11), though ruinous, is of particular interest

IANB F

in view of its situation in the jaws of Upper Strathtay just above the legionary fortress and other Roman works at Inchtuthil. Here the walled inner enclosure, now choked with impenetrable rhododendrons, crowns a rocky bluff; it measures axially only 115 feet by 70 feet. It is very strongly defended by natural hazards and four ramparts.

Region 38 includes the county of Fife, the hill-forts in which are known, and Strathearn, which is by no means so well understood as yet. Nevertheless it can be observed that one quarter of the known hill-forts

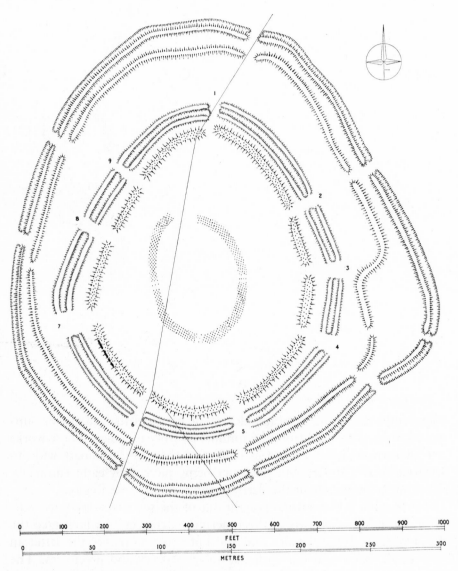

Fig. 10. The Brown Caterthun, Angus.

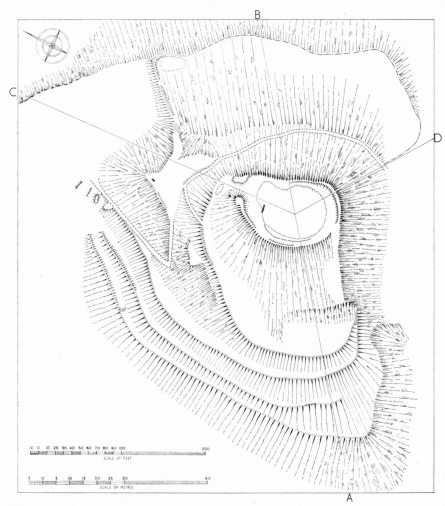

Fig. 11. King's Seat, Dunkeld, Perthshire.

in the Region are oval bivallate works. Among the rest are Forgandenny and Abernethy, and several which are mentioned below in connection with the so-called 'citadels' or defensive enclosures.

The greatest concentrations of hill-forts and large settlements occur south of the Firth of Forth. In Region 32, ninety-six such works out of a total of one hundred and sixteen are oval multivallate structures. In Teviotdale, in Region 34, thirty out of forty are long ridge-forts, such as Kaim Law (fig. 12), of a type not found elsewhere. Several of them contain surface traces of timber houses. This, combined with the simple plan, may suggest that such works fall comparatively early into the assemblage of post-palisade structures.

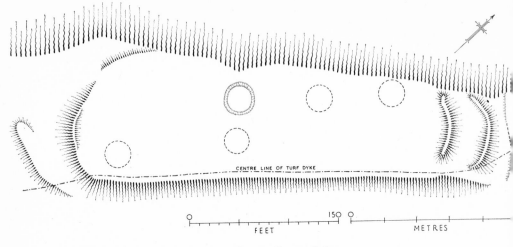

CENTRE LINE OF TURF DYKE

FEET   METRES

Fig. 12. Kaim Law, Roxburghshire. (Crown Copyright)

In the vicinity of Peebles, in the central part of Region 34, twenty-two hill-forts and large settlements occurring in a certain restricted area include among them ten which are provided with a heavy cross-dyke obstructing the easiest line of approach—a feature which is virtually unknown elsewhere. In Region 37, a hundred recorded hill-forts or large settlements include forty-three of the kind locally known as a birren. These impressive works, which do not occur outside the area, are defended by one or two massive rubble ramparts each with a broad external quarry-ditch. A measurement of 70 feet across rampart and ditch is not uncommon.

In Region 36 there are among others twenty-six small, almost sub-rectangular forts, usually consisting of one considerable wall with the additional defence of a rather lesser outer one. Of these twenty-six, eight exhibit vitrifaction, and it is possible that all are of timber-laced construction. At one of them, the Mote of Mark, excavations revealed evidence of occupation at least as early as the first century A.D., and it can be assumed that these little forts may represent, as has been suggested,[18] an element of the Novantae.

Region 36 is also noted for the concentration of about thirty small promontory forts around the coasts flanking the Mull of Galloway and Burrow Head. Virtually nothing is known about any of these, and it is possible that the dates of construction of individual forts may range from some time in the later centuries B.C. to Viking times.[19]

While the hill-forts and promontory forts of Regions 50 and 51 are not as yet thoroughly known, beginnings made in a systematic survey of Argyll and information published in the *Inventory of Skye*, together with facts supplied by the Archaeology Division, Ordnance Survey, indicate a predominance of walled structures over those defended by ramparts. The former include a fairly high proportion of comparatively small multi-vallate oval works and promontory forts, as well as some in the construction of which advantage has been taken of several levels of a naturally terraced crag. There are a few promontory forts of uncertain date but no hill-forts in the Outer Hebrides.

It remains to discuss the incidence and significance of *oppida* and the larger settlements (fig. 13), and the phenomenon of the so-called 'citadels' or defensive enclosures, before attempting conclusions.

Oppida and the Larger Settlements. The largest example of Iron-Age fortification to have been recorded so far in Northern Britain, at Stanwick in Teesdale (Region 29), began as a hill-fort or large settlement 17 acres in extent and continued as a plain-fort of 140 acres which was later expanded to include 750 acres.[20] Such a structure belongs among the great, late *oppida* of which fifty-nine others have been identified in the area of the greater Celtic expansion. Excepting this, the next two largest hill-forts or large settlements are on Traprain Law, East Lothian (Region 33)[21] and Eildon Hill North, Roxburghshire (Region 34), both of about 40 acres extent at their largest. This may be compared with the 45 acres of the final phase at Maiden Castle, Dorset. The importance of these two is paramount. The questions which, so the random finds proclaim, could be answered by properly-conducted excavations on Traprain Law, would be of overriding importance in assisting towards the further elucidation of a whole millennium of pre- and proto-history—the Iron Age and the Roman-British and the pre-Saxon sub-Roman periods of eastern Northern Britain up to the Firth of Forth if not, indeed, to the Firth of Tay.

Considerable interest attaches to the difference in the sizes of the several successive structural phases which preceded the final ones in these *oppida*. At Traprain Law (fig. 14), a primary fortification of no more than an acre or two in extent may have originally succeeded an open Late Bronze settlement, but if so all traces of it have disappeared from the surface. It has been estimated[22] that the first recognisable defensive work enclosed about 10 acres, the next about 20, the third about 30 and the fourth about 40 acres. In the final phase, the area was reduced to about 30 acres. At Eildon Hill North (fig. 15), after a primary enclosure of about 2 acres there followed an expansion to about 9 acres before the final enlargement to 40 acres. While the great majority of the hill-forts and large settlements are small, like Eildon Hill North 1, the occurrence of a certain number of works measuring six or more acres in extent has been recorded.

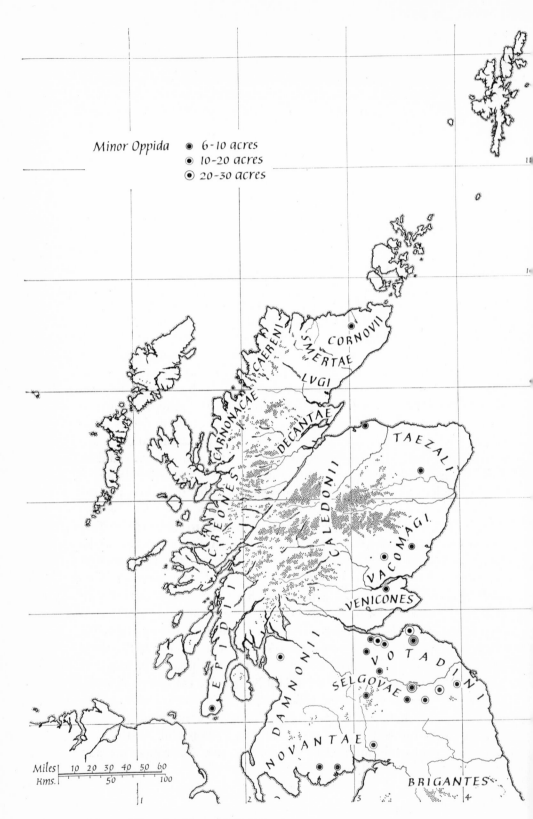

Minor Oppida
   ◉ 6-10 acres
   ◉ 10-20 acres
   ◉ 20-30 acres

CORNOVII
SMERTAE
CAEREN
LVGI
CARNONACAE
DECANTAE
TAEZALI
CREONES
CALEDONII
VACOMAGI
EPIDII
VENICONES
DAMNONII
VOTADINI
SELGOVAE
NOVANTAE
BRIGANTES

Miles 10 20 30 40 50 60
Kms. 50 100

Fig. 13. Minor Oppida and Tribal Names.

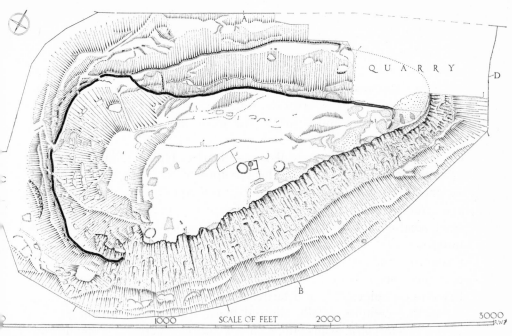

Fig. 14. Traprain Law, East Lothian.

In Greater Tweeddale these are Hownam Law (22 acres); Yevering Bell (13); The Dunion (12); Eildon Hill North 11 and Rubers Law (9); White Meldon (8¾) and Whiteside Rig (6½). All have a single wall and almost all still show abundant surface traces of timber houses. All these minor *oppida* except Yevering Bell and Hownam Law lie, together with numerous hill-forts and large settlements, in what was probably the territory of the Selgovae. It may be permissible to see in them the principal centres of successive stages in the development of the various bands of native peoples and immigrants who eventually merged into the historical Selgovae, with a single 'capital' on Eildon Hill North (40 acres). About 300 house-floors can still be seen on the surface in this *oppidum*, but a large and comparatively flat area in the south part of the enclosure has been ploughed and afforested, and it may be supposed that up to another 200 house-floors at least have been destroyed. With a population amounting to perhaps two or three thousand, it is unlikely that all the able-bodied occupants would have been engaged upon the production of food. It is reasonable to envisage that this capital settlement supported craft-workers and even administrators, and stood in a superior position vis-à-vis the abundant settlements of the rest of the people.

Other substantial hill-forts occur in Regions 32 and 33. Largest is the hill-fort on North Berwick Law, East Lothian, which attains a size of 28 acres although it includes a high proportion of precipitous inhospitable ground. Next comes the enclosure on Salisbury Craigs, Edinburgh, formed by a wall 650 yards long cutting off an area containing 25 acres which is otherwise bounded by the apparently undefended crest of the cliff. Adjacent to this is Arthur's Seat, 20 acres of the summit of which are bounded for the most part by the apparently undefended brinks of steep or precipitous descents and partly by two parallel walls 400 yards long. The final phase in the hill-fort on Kaimes Hill, Midlothian, attains $6\frac{1}{2}$ acres in extent. Thus, in the territory of the Votadini as in that ascribed to the Selgovae, analysis of regional types reveals that ever fewer and larger works were constructed, suggesting the gradual progressive amalgamation and cohesion of several originally independent colonies into some kind of politically stable organisation which the Romans could recognise, And, as in the other case, there is evidence here to suggest that the story can be carried back to a primary Iron-Age settlement based upon homesteads and farms and small settlements.

In the territory usually allowed to the Damnonii (Region 35) the largest hill-fort is on Walls Hill, Renfrewshire ($18\frac{1}{2}$ acres). Timber houses, no traces of which appear on the surface, were found here by excavation.[23] Other important structures in this region are Carman (fig. 16), just north of the River Clyde in Dunbartonshire ($5\frac{1}{2}$ acres), and Duncarnock, Renfrewshire and Dunmore, Stirlingshire, both $4\frac{1}{2}$ acres. Further south, the territory usually assigned to the Novantae includes Annandale and Nithsdale (Region 37) and Wigtownshire and the Stewartry of Kirkcudbright (Region 36). The former area is dominated by Burnswark (17 acres), but it also includes Castle O'er (5 acres). The latter has The Moyle (9 acres) and a work called the Giant's Dyke on Barstobric Hill, formed by a wall 500 yards long which runs from one point on the brink of a steep slope to another to enclose an area of 8 acres.

This brief record of the incidence of the larger hill-forts in the Lowlands, emphasising their comparative rarity and pointing by deduction towards the probable function of at least some of them, can be concluded by notes on a few others. First, it should be remembered that the royal castles at Edinburgh and Stirling occupy sites which were certainly in use early in the first millennium A.D., and probably in pre-Roman times. Each occupies the head of a crag-and-tail feature and each is cut off from approach up the tail by a moat. Assuming that the positions of the moats define the limits of the original defended areas, then Dineidyn[24] would have occupied $6\frac{1}{2}$ acres and Urbs Giudi[25] 4 acres.

The largest work in Region 38, where the Venicones are placed, is

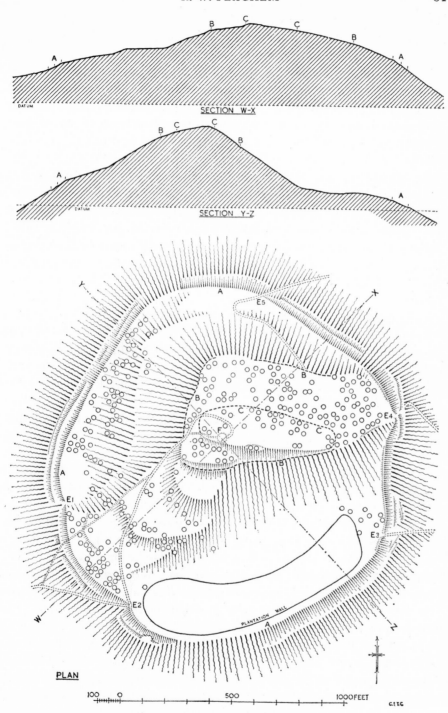

Fig. 15. Eildon Hill North, Roxburghshire. (Crown Copyright)

the last phase on Norman's Law, Fife (10 acres); next in size comes the enclosure crowning the wild summit of Benarty, Fife (5 acres), formed by a wall 450 yards long running in an arc from one point on the cliff bordering the north flank of the hill to another and including some boulders over 6 feet in length in its fabric. The hill-forts on Green Craig (Fife) and Moncrieffe Hill (Perthshire) both attain about 4 acres in extent. In Region 40, among the numerous hill-forts of the Vacomagi, the earliest phase on Turin Hill ($7\frac{1}{2}$ acres) is exceeded only by the unfinished work on Kinpurney Hill ($16\frac{1}{2}$ acres). The Taezali of Aberdeenshire (Region 41) had several substantial works, including most of the large unfinished examples already mentioned; but among the complete hill-forts or large settlements only Tillymuick attains as many as 6 acres. This walled enclosure crowning a low hill in the north part of the Bennachie massif contains surface traces of at least 56 houses with room for as many more. These appear as rings of scattered stones, recalling rather the base of the filling of a cavity wall than the ruined foundation of a solid wall.

The Caledonii, who may or may not originally have extended south of the Grampians, can be assigned much of Region 44, the forts of which are dominated by Burghead ($6\frac{3}{4}$ acres). In the far north, the few hill-forts in Regions 47 and 48, usually assigned to the Cornovii, the Smertae and the Lugi, include as the largest Buaile Oscar, on Beinn Freiceadain ($8\frac{1}{2}$ acres). On the west, in Region 51, there is a large hill-fort on Cnoc Araich ($6\frac{1}{2}$ acres), close to Southend in Kintyre, the territory of the Epidii.

'Citadels' or Defensive Enclosures. In contrast to these larger structures are the works which have been called 'citadels'. These usually have internal axial measurements of about 130 feet by about 100 feet within a wall about 12 feet thick. They occur in apparent association with walls or ramparts enclosing larger areas, but now that examples have been studied in the field wherever they occur, it has become clear that the 'citadels' were constructed at a later date than were the larger fortifications. Further, it appears that in most cases, if not all, the latter were not kept up after the 'citadels' were built, so that the term 'citadel' does not strictly apply. It is important to note that such works occur over a very wide area, including the whole of the Tyne-Forth and Solway-Clyde Provinces as well as the south parts of both the North-Eastern and the Atlantic Provinces. This is a spread which no other recognised type of structure achieved, even in the pioneering days of the all-timber fortifications which are at present somewhat loosely classed.

The choice of a name for works of this class has been difficult. While 'citadel' is clearly misleading, the use of 'ring-fort' is equally so; for not only are almost all of them oval on plan, but the term 'ring-fort' has an established particular meaning in relation to a large class of monuments in Ireland. 'Fortlet' belongs to the Romans, and 'castle', though it has

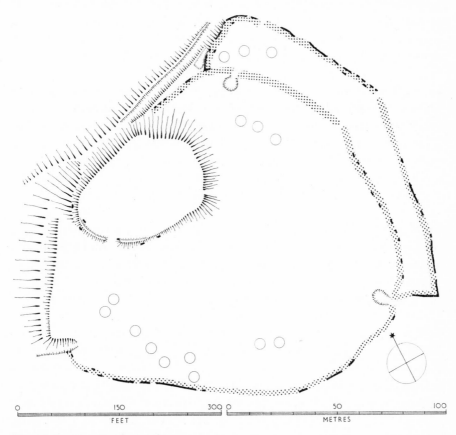

Fig. 16. Carman, Dunbartonshire.

been used in prehistoric contexts, is inappropriate. The term 'defensive enclosure' may serve until a better is produced.

More than a score of defensive enclosures can be recognised—the element of doubt which forbids an exact tally being due to the occurrence of some examples which lie within outworks little bigger than themselves, so that the distinction between them is blurred. About as many as half of the defensive enclosures, however, are associated with examples of the larger hill-forts and minor *oppida* already mentioned, a fact which may be interpreted to show that the status of the earlier works was being sought for the latter. In Region 40, the innermost enclosure on the Brown Caterthun (fig. 10) may be an example, while the circular works on Turin Hill might also belong to this class. Undoubted examples occur in Region 38 on Norman's Law, Green Craig and Moncrieffe Hill; in Region 32 a probable example occurs on Hownam Law; in Region 33 at Craigie Hill, West Lothian (originally 3 acres) and Dalmahoy, Midlothian (originally 4 acres); in Region 34 on Whiteside Rig, Shaw Craigs and Rubers Law; in Region 35 at Carman (fig. 16) and possibly Duncarnock; and in Region 36 at The Moyle. In addition, they are found in such smaller forts as Dumyat, Stirlingshire and Dunearn, Fife, in Region 38; at Chatto Craig and Burnt Humbleton, Roxburghshire, in Region 32; probably at Dowhill, Ayrshire (Region 35) and Holmains, Dumfriesshire (Region 37); probably at Ranachan Hill, Kintyre, and possibly at Cnoc nan Sroine, Mull, in Region 51. Some of these can be seen to overlie the larger fortifications, and so to declare themselves as secondary. At Craigie Hill, Moncrieffe Hill, Norman's Law, Dunearn, Carman, Shaw Craigs and Whiteside Rig, for example, parts of the walls of the defensive enclosures overlie the ruins of the earlier works; and at several other places, such as Green Craig, Dumyat and Dalmahoy they probably do so. If it can be accepted that such works were built after the requirement for the hill-forts and larger settlements had diminished or, more probably, passed altogether, then it remains to attempt to account for them.

Several pointers exist to suggest that these enclosures may have been built late in the period when Roman influence was still exercised at least in parts of Northern Britain, or immediately thereafter. The 'citadel' on Rubers Law contains in the fabric of its wall dressed blocks from a disused Roman building which, it has been assumed, must have dated from the second century A.D. Fragments of moulds and a gold ornament identified as of Early Mediaeval date were found in the example at Dalmahoy. At Moncrieffe Hill, Norman's Law and Carman, round stone-walled houses of a type locally associated with late Roman times occur alongside the defensive enclosures. At Clatchard Craig, Fife, an unusually large defensive enclosure, measuring 240 feet by 100 feet, lay partly in and partly upon the defences of an earlier fort; both are now quarried away, but before this process was completed a Roman dressed stone and relics of Early Mediaeval date were recovered.

Most of the defensive enclosures are situated south of the Firths of Tay and Clyde, the region in which were developed the British Kingdoms of Northumbria and Strathclyde and the Pictish Provinces of Fortrenn and Fib (Strathearn and Mentieth, Fife and Kinross), in Early Mediaeval times. It is suggested that the enclosures may have represented the headquarters of some kind of local administration, or at least overlordship, which developed after the days of hill-forts and *oppida* were done—when possibly such late capitals as the final phase on Traprain

Law were in occupation—before the rectangular timber buildings of the Early Mediaeval period, placed in less arduous situations, came into universal use.

Dundurn and Dunadd. The fortifications at Dundurn, in Perthshire and at Dunadd, Argyll, must be mentioned in this. connection. Both are known from literary evidence to have been in occupation of some sort as late as the seventh century A.D., this being confirmed at Dunadd by relics. But they are also of interest, on two counts. First, they are the most elaborate representatives yet known of hill-forts built on rocky eminences the surfaces of which were diversified by natural terraces. Second, in the course of edging all the terraces with walls, the summits of the two sites, and those of others like them, naturally acquired the status of citadels in the proper sense of the word. The only other solid information about either work is the presence of Roman-British material among the finds from Dunadd.[26] Nevertheless, the overwhelming probability must be that both are basically Early Iron-Age hill-forts, re-used— perhaps sporadically—and possibly repaired or improved by undiscriminating or desperate persons until as late as the seventh century. It has even been suggested that Dunadd was founded by settlers from Ulster[27] —but this can be satisfactorily dismissed: first, because there is no evidence that such hill-forts were still being constructed at the relevant period, even though they might have been undergoing repair or strengthening; and secondly, since no such monuments or works in the remotest degree similar to them were ever built in Ulster.

In the light of the wide researches which have been carried out during the last fifteen years, it is thus possible to confirm that the defensive enclosure is a recognisable and late development, and that it did not form part of a so-called 'citadel-fort'. And it can be proposed that Dunadd and Dundurn represent Early Iron-Age hill-forts the defences of which may have been repaired or improved.[28]

The Pattern of Iron-Age Settlement. The necessity of depending almost entirely upon the evidence provided by field surveys, in default of a sufficient body of evidence from excavations, imposes a narrow limit upon what can be said about those aspects of Iron-Age settlement which the structural remains represent. It may be useful, however, to conclude by examining the broad relationship in which the hill-forts and large settlements, and the homesteads and farms which lie behind and beside them, stand with regard to other contemporary monuments—namely, the non-communal brochs and duns which between them provide the next largest number of extant monuments of the period. The brochs—

dwellings whose remains are solid and heavy enough to render a map of their distribution an unusually reliable version of that often unsatisfactory aid—are distributed over the north and west, in the Atlantic Province. The few examples outside this main distribution do not concern the present argument. Equally well preserved for the same reason are the duns, a category which includes small works built to a preconceived plan—round, oval or sub-rectangular—with thick walls which contain chambers or galleries or both;[29] and, *faute de mieux*, for this general purpose, numerous small walled structures which may have been no more than thick-walled dwellings.[30] The distribution of duns, also mainly but not exclusively in the Atlantic Province, is largely in Regions 50 and 51 (see map at end.)

It is very obvious from the map that the country is quite sharply divided into areas in which hill-forts and large settlements predominate and those in which brochs or duns account for virtually all monuments. In spite of certain overlaps, the forts fall chiefly in the south and east, the brochs in the north and the duns in the west. These distributions, together with considerations of geography, vegetation and tribal groupings, and the regional variations among the hill-forts and large settlements themselves, formed the foundations upon which the proposed division of the four provinces into regions was based.[31]

So little is known of the earlier Iron-Age dwellings in the Atlantic Province that it is as yet difficult to visualise the conditions of settlement pertaining there before the development of the builders of brochs and duns, which may not have taken place much before the turn of the eras. For the present purpose, however, it is sufficient to note that in the period shortly before the arrival of the Romans, before the fundamental changes this brought about even in territories beyond their direct influence, the pattern of settlement throughout Northern Britain was thus and thus. It remains for several future generations to decide upon the origins and the character of the several developing native and immigrant settlements, the monuments of which are all displayed here together.

Notes

1. Based on the Reconnaissance Survey of Scotland and the Survey of England published by the Ordnance Survey in 1953.
2. *PSAS* xciv (1960-1), 79ff.
3. *PSAS* xcii (1958-9), 15ff.
4. The Editor is indebted to the Commissioners for permission to refer to this and other unpublished material from the records of the Royal Commission on the Ancient and Historical Monuments of Scotland.

5. *PSAS* LXXXIII (1948-9), 45 ff.

6. *Arch. Ael.*[4] XXXVII (1959), 217 ff.

7. *PSAS* XCI (1957-8), 61 ff.

8. *PSAS* XXXVI (1901-2), 230.

9. *Problems of the Iron Age in Southern Britain*, ed. S. S. Frere (Occasional Paper No. 11, University of London Institute of Archaeology, 1961), 17; T. C. M. Brewster, *The Excavation of Staple Howe* (Malton, 1963).

10. For Harehope, *PSAS* XCIII (1959-60), 174 ff.; for Woolshears Wood, R.C.A.H.M.(S.), *Peeblesshire* (forthcoming).

11. *PSAS* LXXXIV (1949-50), 126, pl. XIII.2.

12. *Arch. J* CXI (1955), 56, 63, 93, where drawings of a Section and of the Inner Face of the Burghead wall are reproduced.

13. *PSAS* LXXXVI (1951-2), 191-4.

14. Op. cit.

15. It should be noted that Knock of Alves, Denoon Law, Turin Hill and The White Caterthun have been included here although no positive proof that their walls were timber-laced has been adduced.

16. R.C.A.H.M.(S.), *Lorn, Argyll* (forthcoming).

17. V. G. Childe, *The Prehistory of Scotland* (London, 1935), 233.

18. *TD & GNHAS* XXXVIII (1961), 67.

19. Comparable monuments which yielded no dating evidence from soundings occur in Ireland: see *PRIA* Vol. 55, Section C, No. 2 (1952), 25-35, where references are given to promontory forts in Cornwall, Brittany, Antrim and the Isle of Man.

20. Sir M. Wheeler, *The Stanwick Fortifications* (London, 1954).

21. In *The Iron Age in North Britain*, A. L. F. Rivet, *Ant.* XXXVI (1962), 30, the localities pertaining to Regions 33 and 34 have inadvertently been transposed.

22. *PSAS* LXXXIX (1955-6), 284 ff.

23. F. Newall, *Excavations at Walls Hill, Renfrewshire* (Paisley, 1960).

24. The sketch of Edinburgh Castle in 1647 by Gordon of Rothiemay shows what is really no more than a hill-fort with a rather elaborate gateway. R.C.A.H.M.(S.), *The City of Edinburgh*, fig. 67.

25. R.C.A.H.M.(S.), *Stirlingshire*, 37.

26. C. A. R. Radford, in *Dark Age Britain*, ed. D. B. Harden (London, 1956), 63.

27. *The Problem of the Picts*, ed. F. T. Wainwright (Edinburgh, 1955), 81.

28. *TD & GNHAS* XXXVIII (1961), 67.

29. *PSAS* XC (1956-7), 24 ff.

30. *PSAS* XCIII (1959-60), 192 ff.

31. For Provinces, R.C.A.H.M.(S), *Roxburghshire*, 15, 16; for Regions, *Ant.* XXXVI (1962), 29.

Chapter Five

A FIELD SURVEY
IN NORTHUMBERLAND

GEORGE JOBEY

The geographical county of Northumberland, some two thousand square miles in extent, accounts for over one third of the Tyne-Forth Province as defined. The following paper summarises the results of a field survey carried out mainly within the suggested Region 31, so far as it has progressed and falls within the terms of reference for the conference.[1]

Topographical distinctions in the county are clear cut (fig. 1). North of the River Aln, the north-easterly trend of the Cheviots, bordering on the Tweed basin and interrupted only by the north-flowing Till, brings comparatively elevated land to within a few miles of the coast. Hard rocks and gravels of the central block are encircled by sandstone cuesta, running from the east side of the Till to the southern boundaries of Coquetdale. Contrast between the two highland formations is seen to-day in the good, if short, grass of the basic volcanic rocks of the Cheviot slopes and the coarse grass and dark heather moorlands of the peripheral scarps. South of Coquetdale and away from the crag formations the drift cover increases; to the south-east in particular there is in places widespread boulder clay and, despite underlying limestone formations, some areas of poor natural drainage.

(*a*) *Palisaded Enclosures* (figs. 1 and 2). Whatever their precise individual contexts may be in the Early Iron Age or even Late Bronze Age, the recognition of palisaded enclosures by surface indications has been a feature of recent field-work in southern Scotland.[2] As could be anticipated the presence of similar enclosures in Northumberland is well

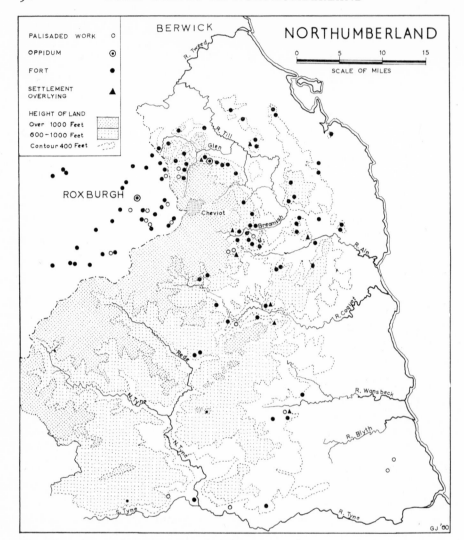

Fig. 1. Distribution of Palisaded Works and Forts.

attested either by field survey or, where the palisades represent an earlier phase beneath later settlements and hill-forts, by excavation. At the moment there is but one known example in County Durham to break the lacuna between Yorkshire and Northumberland, this at West Brandon in Weardale (NZ 201399).[3] Distribution of such sites is widespread and in the Cheviot foothills extends up to and over the twelve-hundred-foot contour. Even so, although the known sites are in well drained situations, natural defence is not a necessary criterion.

As indicated in the first paper, the general nature of the enclosure may be that of a homestead containing a single large round house of

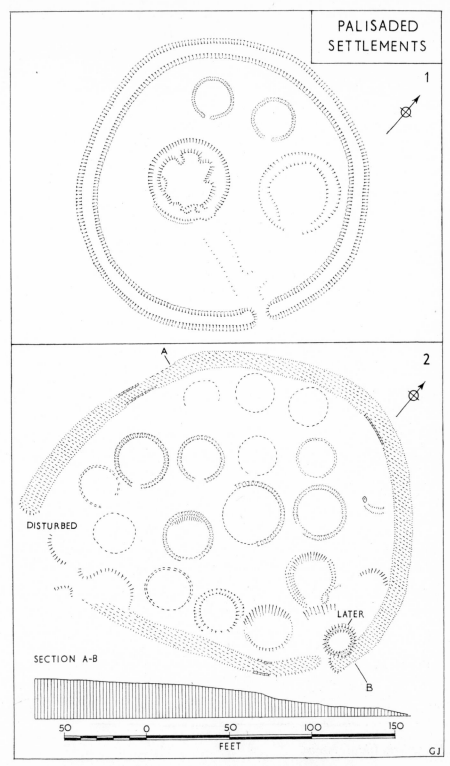

Fig. 2. *Palisaded Settlements: 1, West High Knowe; 2, East High Knowe.*

Little Woodbury[4] or West Plean[5] type, as is found at West Brandon, or a larger settlement of a dozen or more houses, evident, for example, at East High Knowe above the Aln (NT 971125 and fig. 2.2). The shape of the enclosed area varies, being subrectangular at West Brandon, strictly circular at Ingram[6] in the Breamish valley (NZ 012158) or West High Knowe (fig. 2.1), and egg-shaped, dictated by a promontory position, at Huckhoe[7] on the Wansbeck (NZ 073828).

The palisade trenches, cut into rock or subsoil, are either single line, seen at West Sinkside above the College valley (NT 882264), where a small upcast mound still remains on the inside of a trench eighteen

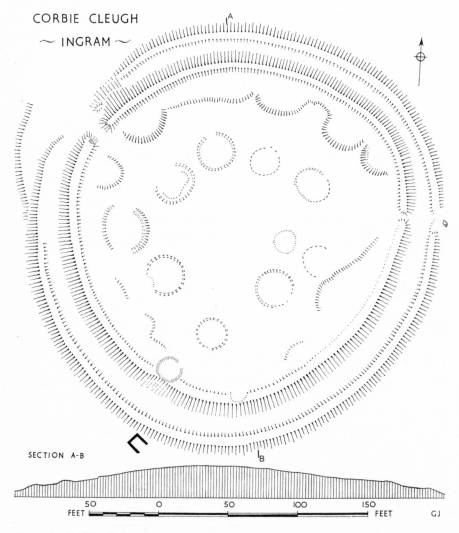

Fig. 3. Corbie Cleugh, Ingram.

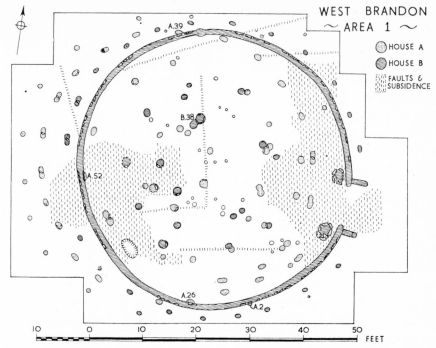

Fig. 4. West Brandon, area 1.

inches wide, or double as in the case of the examples illustrated in fig. 2. Excavation on a number of sites has shown that the trenches were designed to support close-set posts. In the Northumbrian examples distances between the lines of double palisade trenches vary from five to twelve feet, there being no evidence that anything other than upcast from the trenches and perhaps, at the most, brushwood was contained by the two fences. At the entrances, trenches either terminate in large post-holes for the gateways or are conjoined by transverse trenches or 'hairpin' ends. What seems to be an indirect entrance is evident at East High Knowe, a site on which the differential growth of grass caused by the upcast from the palisade trenches marks most of the line of the perimeter (fig. 2.2). A variation in plan, which may be present also on some Scottish sites,[7] occurs at Huckhoe 1,[8] where an inner double palisade and an outer single palisade at a distance of fifty feet apart appear to have been contemporaneous, thus forming inner and outer enclosures. No palisaded settlement has been noted to date in Northumberland identical to that excavated recently at Harehope,[9] Peeblesshire, where fairly widely spaced palisades had been supported in two upcast mounds. On the other hand there are a number of sites, such as that at Corbie Cleugh (NU 013145), where it is difficult to account for the slight nature of the so-called ramparts as being due to later robbing (fig. 3). Whether or not the mounds surrounding this and similar settlements were intended to carry palisades can be resolved only by further excavation.

Circular houses found within the enclosures show some structural variety. At West Brandon where, as often happens, palisades were eventually replaced by ditch and upcast mound, a large house of Little Woodbury type, fifty-eight feet in overall diameter, with main wall, porch, eaves and concentric roof supports represented by individual post-holes, was replaced by a house of similar plan but with a rock-cut trench for a split timber wall (fig. 4). Similar constructional trenches of 'ring-groove' or trench type, as defined in the *Roxburgh Inventory*,[10] prevail as surface features on other Northumbrian settlements. Where the gradient demands it they may be situated on artificially created platforms. The 'ring-ditch' houses of Roxburgh and as excavated at Braidwood,[11] Midlothian, where it was suggested that the post-holes for the house wall lay within a shallow but wide drainage ditch, have not been encountered in quantity in Northumberland. Even so, where they do occur, as in the two large houses at West High Knowe, this explanation is not entirely suited to the surface indications (fig. 2.1). Here the internal platforms are somewhat irregular in shape and the 'ditches' have the appearance of a series of conjoined scoops within the periphery of the houses rather than external drainage gullies similar to those found for example at Draughton, Northants. and Colsterworth, Lincs.[12] The apparent grouping of the 'ring-ditch' and the smaller 'ring-groove' houses at West High Knowe could indicate some difference in status or function. Similar pairing of large and small stone houses is observable on occasions in the walled settlements of later date.[13]

Some interest attaches to the earliest structure found on the site at Brandon. This was a small circular hut of individual post-hole construction, only nineteen feet in diameter, with centre roof support and off-centre hearth, the whole being different in stature and design from the later, large houses of the homestead. The situation is somewhat similar to that found on the homestead at West Plean, Stirling, where it was suggested, on the basis of structural analogies, that the progression from small to large house might represent a transformation of a Late Bronze-Age site by Early Iron-Age traditions.[14]

Small finds from the Northumbrian palisaded sites that have been excavated are not particularly revealing and, in their present paucity, contrast with the quantity of finds from such settlements as Staple Howe,[15] East Yorks. For the moment associated metal-work is absent, and the affinity of the small amount of pottery lies with that from the settlements at Hownam Rings and Hayhope Knowe, Roxburgh.[16] The possibility of a mixed economy exists at Brandon in the presence of saddle querns, iron slag and at least two bowl furnaces for smelting local iron ore.[17] The proximity of cairnfields to palisaded settlements and hill-forts alike in Northumberland is worthy of note.[18] In the circumstances a systematic exploration might have some merit.

Replacement of the palisades enclosing homesteads and settlements by ditch and mound or wall is a well-known phenomenon, occurring in Highland and Lowland Zones alike, and needs no elaboration at this point (e.g. p. 63, Horsburgh). To date only four examples are known by excavation in Northumberland and Durham[19] but the occurrence is obviously a common one. There is no evidence from the Northumbrian sites that this was the occasion for any real change in basic culture. Although the need for additional protection even on the smaller sites was clearly responsible for this development, which doubtless coincides with the earliest phase of hill-fort building, the topographical situation alone of sites like Brandon and Ingram precludes them from being described as hill-forts. In the few areas of Northumberland where palisaded sites and hill-forts can still be observed in close proximity to each other, individual palisaded settlements may at times achieve greater altitude, but it is the position with the strongest natural defence that, with good reason, is selected for the most developed fortification.

(b) *Hill-Forts* (figs. 1, 5, 6, 7). An analysis of the hill-forts over a wide area of North Britain is given in the preceding paper. In the main, the hill-forts of Northumberland are comparable to those of Roxburgh and Lower-Tweeddale with which north Northumberland at least has physical links. The enclosed areas are generally small by southern standards, many not exceeding three hundred feet in internal diameter. Houses when visible and contemporary are similar to those already described. Perhaps house platforms are more frequent but this no doubt is due to the presence of steeper gradients. As in Roxburgh most sites fall within the broad category of contour forts, whilst the sharp scarps east of the Till and south of the Coquet present situations for the so-called cliff and promontory sites such as that at Old Bewick[20] (NU 075216). The distinction is topographical rather than structural. It is apparent that some multivallation could derive from 'downward' construction where the gradient merits it.[21] Similarly, on the hard rocks and where stone is plentiful, solid stone walls faced and terraced out from the hillsides take the place of ditches and upcast. In at least two instances, Brough Law (NT 998164) and Greaves Ash[22] (NT 965163) above the Breamish, the stone ramparts have a double outer face as observed on the hill-fort at Rink Hill,[23] Selkirkshire.

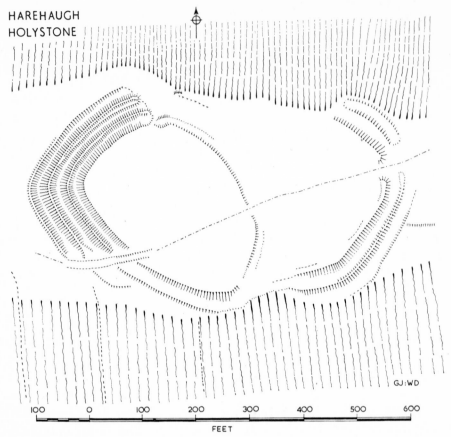

HAREHAUGH
HOLYSTONE

GJ:WD

100   0   100   200   300   400   500   600

FEET

Fig. 5. Harehaugh, Holystone.

Although a number of hill-forts remain to be surveyed in north Northumberland, it is clear that the majority in the county, as in Roxburgh, are multivallate structures at least in their final form. Some, such as Harehaugh in upper Coquetdale (NY 970988) show a single line defence superseded by multivallate defences, as established at Hownam Rings (II and III) and other sites in southern Scotland (fig. 5). Within the multivallate group are a number of bivallate sites enclosed by stone walls or ditches and mounds, situated on hill-tops or in promontory positions, having an outer rampart subsidiary to the inner in size and diverging towards a staggered entrance (e.g. Great Hetha (NT 885275), Greaves Ash, Brough Law and Blawearie[24] (NU 088219)). Although the distance between the two ramparts at the entrance is not excessive and seldom achieves one hundred feet, it is in general sufficient to distinguish such sites temporarily from those forts in similar positions but with close-set ramparts and ditches. It should be stated that the distinction is by no means so marked or well established as in the case of the large hill-forts of southern and south-western England.[25] Moreover, on the small site at Huckhoe II,[26] a similar bivallate plan was determined by that of the underlying palisaded enclosure which it replaced without a break in occupation. And in this connection too, it is worth recalling the small palisaded work on Fasset Hill,[27] Roxburghshire, where the 'horn-works' are once again reminiscent of the more substantial entrances to

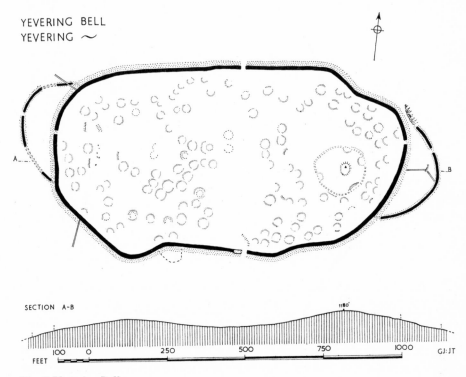

YEVERING BELL
YEVERING ~

SECTION A-B

Fig. 6. Yevering Bell.

some hill-forts. It could be that the defensive plans of some hill-forts merely follow an earlier tradition in a new medium.

The largest hill-fort in Northumberland and one that on northern standards might just qualify to be regarded as an *oppidum* is that at Yevering Bell (NT 928293), where there is an enclosed area of thirteen acres (fig. 6). There are some one hundred and thirty house sites visible within the stoutly built stone rampart, the majority being of platform type with, on occasions, ring-grooves denoting timber walls. A few fragments of ostensible Roman material, obtained from the initial excavations a century ago,[28] suggest that there could be occupation during that period. On the other hand, there appear to be few stone foundations for houses such as are normal in Romano-British settlements in the area and the true extent of such an occupation must be in question. The ditch, as it is described in the original excavations, or palisade trench, as it appears on the ground, which surrounds the summit awaits elucidation but appears to be earlier than some of the house platforms. The annexes

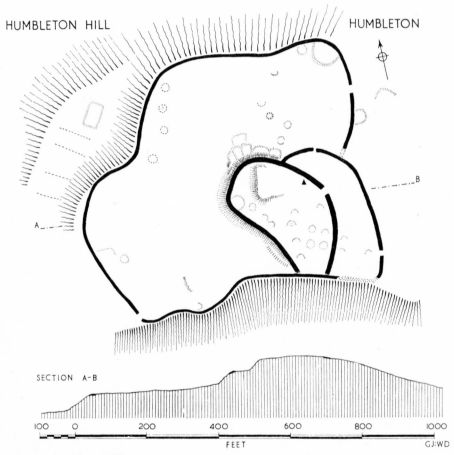

Fig. 7. Humbleton Hill.

can be paralleled on a number of sites in Roxburgh.[29] It is noticeable that the larger sites bordering on the Tweed and its tributaries, found on Eildon Hill, Rubers Law I, Hownam Law[30] and Yevering Bell, occur at intervals of ten to fourteen miles.

Somewhat unusual in Northumberland is the fort on Humbleton Hill (NT 967283) overlooking the Till and the Glen, with its stoutly walled central enclosure and less strongly walled but extensive annexes (fig. 7). The nearest parallels in Roxburghshire are the forts at Burnt Humbleton and Chatto Craig[31] and it could be that the site on Humbleton

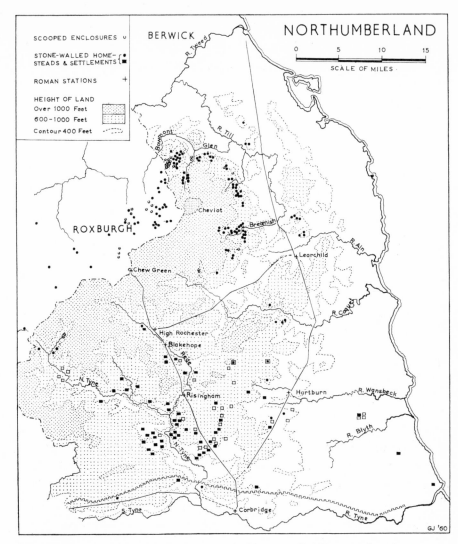

Fig. 8. Distribution of Scooped Enclosures and of Stone-walled Homesteads and Settlements.

Hill will fall within the category of citadel forts. Nevertheless, the few house-types that are visible have been of timber, denoted by platforms and circular grooves, and are similar to those at Yevering Bell and in the smaller contour forts.

Even when allowance is made for the effect of subsequent differences in land utilisation, it seems clear that the weight of distribution of fortified sites lies to the north of the Coquet and, incidentally, the line of the later Roman cross route between Dere Street and the Devil's Causeway (figs. 1 and 8). Strong multivallate defences in particular are not frequent

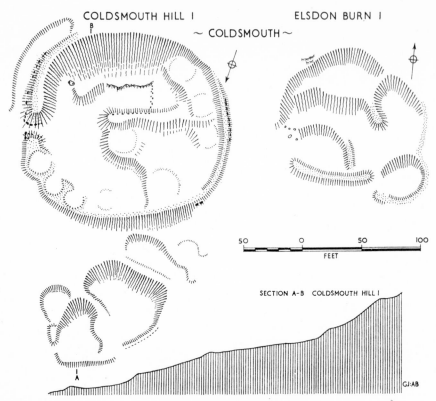

Fig. 9. Scooped Enclosures: Coldsmouth Hill I and Elsdon Burn I.

in the southern parts of the county. The lack of works of any strength is noticeable too in North Tynedale and adjacent parts of Liddesdale in Roxburghshire. No more than a preliminary investigation has been made in County Durham but hill-forts are relatively scarce,[32] a situation shared with parts of Brigantia generally.

(*c*) *Scooped Enclosures* (figs. 8 and 9). Before turning to stone built settlements of the Roman Iron Age, it will be as well to consider briefly the so-called scooped enclosures, long recognised as a type of site in southern Scotland.[33] In short, they consist of a series of scoops and platforms lying within a stone enclosure wall or mound, generally situated on hill-slopes above the valley floor in non-defensive positions. Many bear a general physical resemblance to some of the Late Bronze-Age settlement sites in southern England.[34] Twenty years ago excavation of one such site in Peeblesshire[35] yielded evidence of occupation in the fifteenth and sixteenth centuries and a late mediaeval date has continued to be associated with them, though the fact that some contained hut-circles, indicated by shallow scoops or stone foundations, did not escape notice.[36]

The distribution of such sites in south-eastern Scotland can be seen to extend into Northumberland by way of the valleys of the Bowmont, Till, Breamish and Coquet. There are also two recorded examples situated above the Kielder Burn in North Tynedale (fig. 8). The most significant feature about the Northumbrian examples is the occurrence of floors ostensibly to accommodate round timber houses and, in some instances, the presence of circular stone houses in apparently secondary contexts. This can be seen for example at a site on Coldsmouth Hill (NT 857293), one of a series of ten unrecorded sites lying in a half mile stretch near to Bowmont Water (fig. 9). Here in the uphill enclosure, circular stone houses have been constructed from the material of the enclosure wall, whereas circular floors for timber houses can be traced elsewhere in the enclosure. What is conceivably a transitional stage between scooped enclosure and that type of walled settlement current in a Romano-British context, can be seen also at Staw Hill (NT 885299), where both shallow scoops for house floors and round stone houses front on to a levelled courtyard. The size of these scooped enclosures varies, as with other sites, between homesteads of a single enclosed scoop containing perhaps one slight platform and larger settlements with numerous scoops and floors often separated by unexcavated ridges.

Although temporary or even permanent reoccupation of such enclosures at a late date can be anticipated in areas where suitable habitation sites are at a premium, it is suggested that the scooped enclosure itself can best be seen as a forerunner of the Romano-British walled settlement which it resembles so closely. No examples have been excavated in Northumberland[37] and none to date has appeared in physical contact with an Iron-Age hill-fort, though a possible example, together with a walled settlement of stone houses, overlies the multivallate hill-fort at Kirkton Hill[38] in Roxburghshire. The full distribution of such enclosures in the northern area has not been worked out and attention might be directed for example to some of the Dumfriesshire 'birrens'.[39] Physically, the scooping is probably no more than a constructional adaptation to a particular type of terrain.

(d) *Stone-walled Homesteads and Settlements* (figs. 8, 10, 11). The relatively late appearance of the enclosed and compact groups of circular stone houses in the Tyne-Forth Province has been demonstrated by the frequency with which they can be seen to overly the defences of pre-Roman hill-forts.[40] The extent of the phenomenon in Northumberland is more striking than the few published examples such as Greaves Ash and Lordenshaws[41] (NZ 054993) would suggest, with stone houses and

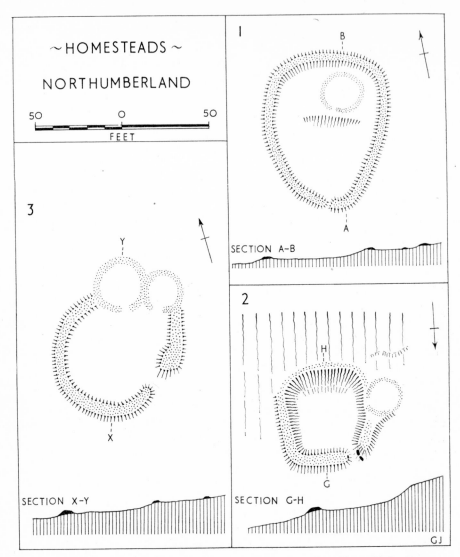

Fig. 10. Typical stone-walled Homesteads: 1, Ells Knowe; 2, Hartside; 3, Elsdon Burn.

courtyards generally taking advantage of the protection afforded by the lee slopes. In other instances, as at Jenny's Lantern, Bolton (NU 109152), the close proximity of non-defensive walled settlement and abandoned hill-fort, although there is no physical contact between the two, no doubt points to the same sequence. Similar homesteads and settlements not necessarily in close proximity to hill-forts form one of the largest classes of extant field remains in the county. Datable evidence from these sites, on both sides of the present Border, ranges from at least the second to

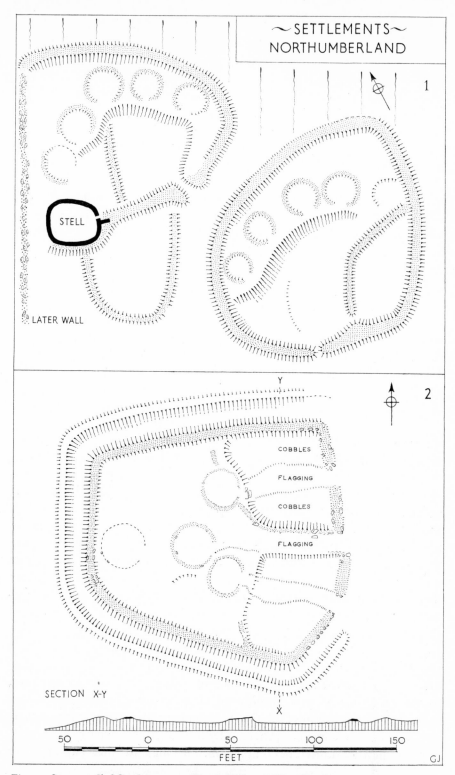

SETTLEMENTS
NORTHUMBERLAND

1

STELL

LATER WALL

Y

2

COBBLES

FLAGGING

COBBLES

FLAGGING

SECTION X-Y

X

50   0   50   100   150
FEET

GJ

Fig. 11. Stone-walled Settlements: 1, Knock Hill; 2, Riding Wood.

the fourth century A.D. and, in two instances, into the post-Roman period.[42]

The sites can be considered briefly within two main geographical areas (fig. 8). First those north of the River Coquet, where they are situated mainly on the slopes of the deeply cut valleys of the Cheviot foothills, generally below the one-thousand-foot contour line. When found near to earlier palisaded settlements as at High Knowe (NT 976122) less exposed positions have clearly been selected, possibly in response to a changed climate or natural cover.

In the homestead category there is the small circular or oval site with a substantial wall, sometimes orthostatic, completely enclosing one or two houses which face on to a scooped or levelled forecourt (fig. 10, no. 1). This homestead type is familiar from the excavations at Crock Cleuch[42] in Roxburghshire, where there was a possible span of occupation from the second century A.D. into the post-Roman period, which in turn led to a comparison with the description of St Cuthbert's dwelling on the Farne.[43] What are probably no more than variations on a theme appear also in Northumberland in the form of no. 3 where the enclosure walls spring from the house walls in a manner reminiscent of some courtyard houses of North Wales and Cornwall; or no. 2, found on steeper slopes, where the house is not poised uphill but situated to one side so as to reduce the difference in level between it and the courtyard.

Of more frequent occurrence than the simple homestead is the larger oval shaped settlement containing half a dozen houses or so fronting on to the yard, the latter occasionally divided as at Knock Hill in the Breamish Valley (NT 999173; fig. 11, no. 1). Even larger settlements arise either by direct additions to an original nucleus thereby utilising existing walls, as at Greaves Ash, or by a loose collection of homesteads and settlements in very close proximity to each other, as on Hartside in the same valley (NT 985156). No social implications are necessarily foreseen in the detached and semi-detached establishments. The largest settlement of round stone houses in the county is at Greaves Ash where there are some thirty extant buildings. When allowance is made for imponderables, such as desertion and reconstruction over a long period of time, this may not be large. On the other hand, in an area of approximately two square miles in the same valley there is a total of some one hundred and fifty enclosed round houses with stone foundations. They are prolific in other areas of the Cheviots too, for instance that behind Yevering, there perhaps with some import for later history. There is a general reduction in the number of these settlements on the acid moorlands peripheral to the Cheviots, where at least to-day the stock carrying capacity is somewhat limited in comparison. Although attached paddocks are sometimes found, developed field systems do not appear to be associated with the sites as surveyed. Cultivation terraces and field boundaries do occur in close proximity but their association seems to lie rather with the intrusive and overlying rectangular farm buildings of later date.

There is a basic resemblance between the Cheviot sites and the enclosed hut groups of other hill areas, seen to advantage for example in the latest *Caernarvonshire Inventories*, but this in itself is no argument for an Antonine transfer of population to North Wales from the Tyne-Forth area as once suggested.[44]

Further to the south in Northumberland, in the lands bordering the Wansbeck, North Tyne and Rede, in a zone twelve to fifteen miles wide to the north of the Hadrianic frontier, settlements are again prolific but are almost exclusively rectangular in shape (fig. 11.2).[45] Whilst some enclosures are doubtless of more recent origin and others are not sufficiently well preserved to lend themselves to reliable classification, some forty-five out of one hundred and forty known rectilinear sites can be placed firmly within the category under discussion.

Uniformity in planning is a striking feature of these settlements. Within the walled enclosure the front portion of each site is generally occupied by two yards, lying on either side of a central causeway which is often paved. At the rear lie circular stone houses generally less than six in number. Yards are sometimes hollowed and in excavation cobbled after the fashion of the stockyards of present-day local farms. A shallow ditch frequently surrounds the site with the upcast thrown to the outside. This has led to some settlements being classified as multivallate sites,[46] but is misleading since there appears to be no real intention to fortify and they are situated in positions of little natural strength. In fact there is a close correlation between the ditched settlements and areas of boulder clay drift, whereas those without ditches lie on rocks or gravels. The intention need be no more than that of drainage.

Expansion has taken place on some settlements, but this is generally confined to an increase in the number of houses within the original enclosure walls, and units do not attain the size of some of the Cheviot sites. Even so, their frequency is comparable. In places on the riverine spurs of North Tynedale settlements occur regularly about a quarter of a mile apart, almost as if the extent of landholding on the river frontage had been determined by the intervening tributary streams. However, as with the Cheviot settlements, there are to date no field systems that can be unequivocally associated with them.

Topographical conditions set a limit to the distribution of these settlements to the west of the North Tyne, also demarcated in another context by the line of the linear earthwork known as the Black Dyke. Beyond this lies an area still one of the least densely populated in England. In the upper reaches of the North Tyne, the rectangular shaped sites give way abruptly to the Cheviot type near to the present Border line in the Kielder forest. Recent discoveries of comparable rectilinear settlements on the coastal plain at Tynemouth (NZ 354705) and probably Stannington[47] (NZ 220815) point to a distribution extending across the heavier soils of the south-eastern part of the county, thereby lending strength to the possibility that a good number of the intervening unclassified sites will prove to be of the same type.

Datable evidence from these settlements, such as it is, falls generally within the Antonine period, with a few pieces possibly earlier.[45] The sample is too small to postulate any destruction at the end of the second century in the disasters that befell the frontier. Structural and cultural evidence from excavations gives no support to the connection between these settlements and Rhaetian auxiliaries or settlers, as once mooted.[48] Indeed, apart from the rectangular shape and general orderliness, which could be attributed to Roman influence, they obviously exhibit many of the features of the Cheviot sites.

Before the Hadrianic establishment of the second century the emphasis on Roman military strength had probably already passed to the west and, as is well known, the Hadrianic scheme did not involve outpost forts in the east. In the Antonine reorganisation there was a newly sited fort at Risingham and that at High Rochester was reoccupied (fig. 8). Although details of the military treatment of the Northumberland plain are not yet resolved, it is possible that the whole area was relatively lightly garrisoned as compared with some of the western routes. Against a background such as this, it may be possible to envisage the numerous rectilinear settlements as representing a development, either spontaneous or directed, of a comparatively lightly populated area lying well within the new Antonine frontier and perhaps administered from such forts as Risingham.[49] Or, if one considers an earlier development possible,[50] then, in view of the whole basic concept of the frontier zone and the known regulations imposed upon other frontiers at a later date,[51] the fairly compact distribution of these sites, generally not encroaching within a distance of three miles from the frontier line, could be a reflection of rules imposed from the very start of the Hadrianic system. The number of walled settlements in the territorial area of the Votadini in general, and in parts of Roxburghshire and Northumberland in particular, is striking. Recently attention has been drawn to the possible political implications of the apparent absence of such settlements from Selkirkshire.[52] It would be useful to have a picture of the extent of the comparable settlements of the Romano-British period in Dumfriesshire and the west.

There are only two rectilinear sites, apparently native by elimination, that are heavily defended. Both Manside Cross (NY 985920) and Ewesley Plantation (NZ 050926) have strong multiple ditches and ramparts, and, fortuitously or not, lie between Dere Street and the Devil's Causeway, closing off the area between the forts at Risingham and Hartburn (fig. 8). The possibility of out-stationed territorial patrols as a feature of later frontier history has been discussed elsewhere,[53] and perhaps some para-military status could be envisaged for these two sites. Although excavation over two seasons at Manside Cross has shown revetted and palisaded ramparts and circular stone houses in the interior, the sum total of datable material is confined to two fragments of Romano-British cooking pot.[54] This may serve as a reminder not only of the difficulties involved in attempting to place sites, often at the 'vanishing point of Romanisation', within the established chronology of the frontier area, but also of the main problem involved in excavation on smaller sites in the Highland Zone. Even so, one hopes that time spent in reconnaissance is seldom wasted.

Postscript

The following more detailed surveys have been published since 1961, when this summary was written, and are not referred to in the notes: 'Enclosed stone built Settlements in North Northumberland', *Arch. Ael.*[4] XLII (1964), 41-64; 'Hill Forts and Settlements in Northumberland' *Arch. Ael.*[4] XLIII (1965), 21-64.

Notes

1. Some 350 earthworks have been surveyed to date. Plans, so far as possible at a uniform scale, are available in the Department of Extra-Mural Studies, King's College, Newcastle upon Tyne. It is the intention to publish detailed accounts and lists locally as sections of the survey are completed. A fairly comprehensive list of earthworks prepared by A. H. A. Hogg exists in *PSAN*[4] XI (1946-50), 140-79.
2. E.g. R.C.A.H.M., *Roxburgh*, I and II.
3. J. K. St Joseph, *Cambridge University Air Photo.* DS/O. Excavation report *Arch. Ael.*[4] XL (1962), 1ff.
4. G. Bersu, *PPS* VI (1940), 30ff.
5. K. A. Steer, *PSAS* LXXXIX (1955-6), 231.
6. A. H. A. Hogg, *Arch. Ael.*[4] XX (1942), 110ff. and XXXIV (1955), 150ff.
7. E.g. Morton Mains Hill, Dumfries., R. W. Feachem, *TD & GAS* XXXIII (1954-5), 58ff.

8. G. Jobey, *Arch. Ael.*[4] XXXVII (1959), 224.

9. R. W. Feachem, *PSAS* XCIII (1959-60), 174ff.

10. Vol. I, 19.

11. R. B. K. Stevenson, *PSAS* LXXXIII (1948-9), 1ff.

12. W. F. Grimes in *Problems of the Iron Age in S. Britain*, 21 and 24.

13. E.g. *History of Northumberland*, XV, 79.

14. K. A. Steer, *PSAS* LXXXIX (1955-6), 231.

15. T. C. M. Brewster, *The Excavation of Staple Howe, 1963*.

16. C. M. Piggott, *PSAS* LXXXII (1947-8), 193ff., and LXXXIII (1948-9), 45ff.

17. Cf. iron slag from palisade trenches at Ingram Hill; A. H. A. Hogg, op. cit.

18. E.g. Witchy Neuk in *History of Northumberland*, XV, 28.

19. Brandon, Huckhoe, Ingram Hill, and probably Witchy Neuk (NY 982994) in *Arch. Ael.*[4] XVI (1939), 129ff.

20. Plan in *History of Northumberland*, XIV, 38.

21 A. L. F. Rivet in Frere (ed.), *Problems of Iron Age in S. Britain*, 31.

22. G. Tate, *H. Berwick. N.C.* 1858-62, 295ff. and A. H. A. Hogg, *Ant.* XVII (1943), 139.

23. R.C.A.H.M., *Selkirk*, no. 122.

24. Plan in *History of Northumberland*, XIV, 36.

25. Aileen Fox in *Problems of the Iron Age in S. Britain*, 35ff.

26. *Arch. Ael.*[4] XXXVII (1959), 224.

27. R.C.A.H.M., *Roxburgh*, II, no. 660.

28. G. Tate, *H Berwick NC* 1858-62, 43ff.

29. R.C.A.H.M., *Roxburgh*, I, 18.

30. Ibid., I and II, nos. 597, 145, 299.

31. Ibid., nos. 1040 and 305.

32. The most southerly recorded possibility of multivallate defence in Durham seems to be Shakerton Hill, nr. Bishop Auckland, H. MacLauchlan, *Watling Street*, Sheet II.

33. Summary in R.C.A.H.M., *Roxburgh*, I, 48. Report on similar sites in Northumberland, *Arch. Ael.*[4] XL (1962), 47ff.

34. E.g. Itford Hill, G. P. Burstow and G. A. Holleyman, *PPS* XXIII (1957), 167ff.

35. R. B. K. Stevenson, *PSAS* LXXV (1940-1), 92ff. See also *PSAS* LXXXI (1946-7), 158ff.

36. R.C.A.H.M., *Roxburgh*, I, 48.

37. A bun-shaped rotary quern was found during survey of a possible example at Earles Whin, Wooler (NT 984269).

38. R.C.A.H.M., *Roxburgh*, I, no. 148.

39. R.C.A.H.M., *Dumfries.*, liv f.

40. E.g. K. A. Steer in Richmond (ed.), *Roman and Native in N. Britain*, 98, fig. 2.

41. *History of Northumberland*, XIV, 368 and XV, 30.

42. Crock Cleuch in Roxburgh., *PSAS* LXXXI (1946-7), 138ff., and Huckhoe in Northumberland, op. cit.

43. I. A. Richmond, *Ant.* XV (1941), 88.

44. E.g. W. J. Hemp, *Ant.* XVIII (1944), 191.

45. For more detailed report see G. Jobey, *Arch. Ael.*⁴ XXXVIII (1960), 1ff.

46. A. H. A. Hogg, *Proc. Soc. Ant. Newcastle*, XI (1946-50), 140ff.

47. *Arch. Ael.*⁴ XLI (1963), 19ff. and forthcoming.

48. A. H. A. Hogg, *Ant.* XVII (1943), 136ff.

49. Where there was a *beneficiarius* possibly charged with the supervision of frontier traffic or a market, at least in the third century. *History of Northumberland*, XV, 137.

50. See e.g. re-examination of evidence from Milking Gap, J. P. Gillam in Richmond (ed.), *Roman and Native in N. Britain*, 63.

51. E.g. Cassius Dio, LXXIII, 2 and 3.

52. R.C.A.H.M., *Selkirk*, 21.

53. E.g. I. A. Richmond in *Roman and Native in N. Britain*, 112ff.

54. Excavation not completed.

Chapter Six

FORTS, BROCHS AND WHEEL-HOUSES
IN NORTHERN SCOTLAND

J. R. C. HAMILTON

Ever since the classic studies made by Joseph Anderson in the seventies and eighties of the last century, the broch towers of Northern Scotland have been identified as the strongholds of tightly-knit Iron-Age communities engaged in agriculture, husbandry, reiving and piracy, their occupation being dated to the first centuries of our era on the evidence of imported Roman finds.[1]

For almost fifty years the brochs were practically synonymous in archaeological literature with the Iron Age of this northernmost province embracing Sutherland, Caithness, the Orkney and Shetland Islands and the Western Isles (map at end). Within their shadow subsidiary structures came to light such as the villages of stone-built huts clustered round the towers at Lingro,[2] Midhowe[3] and Gurness[4] in Orkney (pl. 1) and the Keiss brochs in Caithness.[5] Owing to the apparently homogeneous character of the pottery and other finds, their relation to the towers could not be easily defined and they were thought at first to house the dependents of the broch builders. Later, however, it became apparent from the occurrence of similar structures inside the towers and from the presence of late Roman coins, Pictish symbols and relics from Celtic monasteries in the west that their occupation could span several hundred years to the eighth and even ninth century A.D. The broch period of heavily built defences had evidently given way to generally peaceful conditions in which small, open settlements, often built of stone pillaged from the towers, could thrive in comparative isolation.

The origin of the towers was a much more difficult problem to resolve and in recent years two schools of thought have claimed attention. The first, which for convenience may be called the Scottish school and whose most distinguished exponent was the late Gordon Childe, saw the broch as the finest expression—the apogee—of Iron-Age castle architecture.[6] Circular in plan, with a solid ring wall at base surrounding a central court with single passage entrance and mural chambers, the broch consists of an inner and outer casement wall rising from first-floor level, bonded together at intervals by transverse slabs with a staircase leading to wall-top level (pl. 1 and fig. 2, C5). The interior face possesses one or more scarcement ledges or courses to support the floors of a timber range (pl. 2). Doorways from the first or second floor of such ranges could lead through the inner casement to the galleries connected with the staircase.

Already in 1928 the Royal Commission on Ancient Monuments and Historical Buildings in Scotland, after comparing the structural details in the brochs and the stone-built forts further south, tentatively suggested that the towers had developed from the 'galleried duns' of the west coast—both possessing hollow-wall construction and both exhibiting a common tradition in mural cells, bar-holes, door-jambs and battered wall faces.[7] Conclusive proof, however, was lacking and critics claimed that the galleried duns might well represent a late degeneration of castle architecture.

In 1947, this impasse, which had been recognised for some years, was overcome to the satisfaction of the school whose principal spokesman was Sir Lindsay Scott. After studying small domestic structures such as aisled round-houses and wheel-houses in the Hebrides, Sir Lindsay derived the brochs together with these domestic dwellings from the timbered round hut of southern Britain.[8] The transformation, according to this theory, was brought about by a wave of southern refugees, related to the Glastonbury lake villagers, penetrating up the west coast of Scotland, who adapted their dwellings to stone construction in a treeless zone. The evolution of the towers was not to be sought in a pre-broch fort sequence so much as in these domestic structures which Sir Lindsay divided into four classes—the first three of which he regarded as heavily defended farmsteads evolving to the fourth class which alone achieved true tower proportions.[9]

Obviously, with such divergent views prevailing on the military or domestic origin of the towers any final solution could only be achieved by further excavation. The difficulty was to find sites on which earlier Iron-Age occupation could be confirmed and examined. Fortunately, such a site had been discovered in the decade before the Second World War at Jarlshof close to the southernmost tip of the Shetland Islands.[10] In the excavations carried out by the Ministry of Works between 1949

Pl. 1a (above) Broch of Gurness, Aikerness, Orkney, surrounded by secondary buildings flanking paved street; b (below) Broch of Mousa, Shetland, showing basal batter, regular coursing of masonry, single entrance and double casement construction (top). (both Crown Copyright)

Pl. 2 Broch of Mousa, Shetland. Interior view showing two scarcements for support of floors of timber-framed range round the central court. (Crown Copyright)

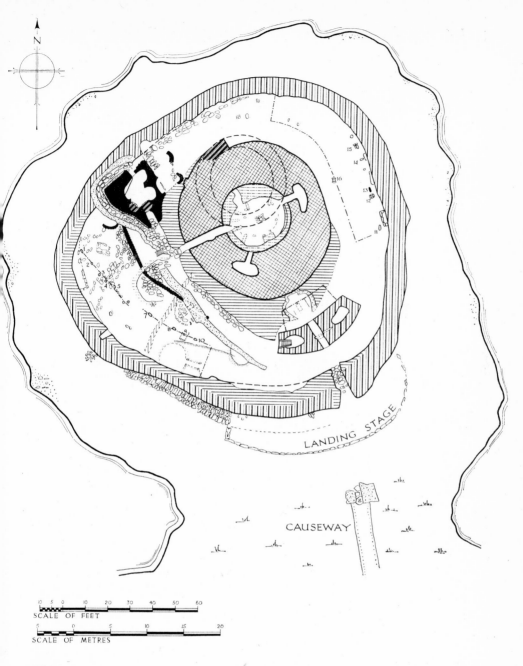

LANDING STAGE

CAUSEWAY

SCALE OF FEET
SCALE OF METRES

◼ LATE BRONZE AGE

▨ IRON AGE I

▥ RINGWALL PERIOD I

▤ RINGWALL PERIOD II

▩ BROCH PERIOD

▦ WHEELHOUSE EARLY

▨ WHEELHOUSE LATE

---- RANGES

Fig. 1. Plan of Clickhimin.

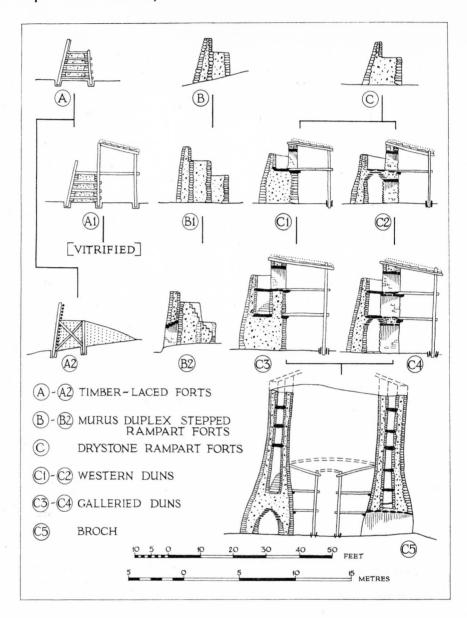

Fig. 2. *Evolution of Iron-Age Fortification Techniques.*

A, B, C *illustrate three basic methods of rampart construction:* A, *Timber-laced Rampart* (*Preist Type*); B, Murus duplex *or* Stepped Rampart; C, *Drystone-built Wall Rampart.*

A1. *Preist type with peripheral timbered range. On destruction by fire results in Dun Troon-Finavon-Rahoy vitrified forts.*

A2. *Hollingbury rampart in Southern Britain.*

and 1951, however, it was found that prior to the building of the broch tower the site had been abandoned and covered by wind-blown sand, over three feet of sterile sandblow separating the earlier Iron-Age occupation levels from the broch horizon. Nevertheless, ceramic evidence[11] suggested that an earlier broch phase might be represented on sites further north, and in 1953 excavation began on the islet broch of Clickhimin twenty-two miles to the north of Jarlshof (pl. 3).

Here a pre-broch sequence was confirmed including important fortifications erected during the missing period at Jarlshof (fig. 1). As these structures were excavated it became apparent that they not only threw light upon the origin of the later towers but on Iron-Age fortification techniques in general. The advances achieved can be briefly summarised:

(1) A pre-broch fort was identified and excavated. It illustrates a type of fortification from which the brochs developed.

(2) The excavation of the interior of the fort allowed basic principles to be defined which governed the development of Iron-Age fortifications not only in the far north but also in other parts of Britain.

(3) Finally a chronological sequence was established for the Iron Age in the Shetland Islands. The evidence confirmed the supposition that whereas the Islands were not the original home of the brochs, they formed an important colony of the broch culture at the beginning of our era.

This sequence will be dealt with in detail in a forthcoming publication[12] and need only be briefly summarised in this paper. At both Jarlshof and Clickhimin, the sites were settled by Late Bronze-Age farmers building oval cubicled houses of stone ultimately derived from the Neolithic type present at Jarlshof and more fully explored by Calder in recent years.[13] It may well prove that the deterioration of climate in the first half of the first millennium B.C. caused the upland farms to be abandoned and coastal sites such as the two under review to be occupied.[14] At Jarlshof

---

B-B2. Murus duplex *or stepped rampart exemplified in the Alpes Maritimes: Castelleras de la Malle, Subeyra, Camp Barlet, etc.; in Central Gaul: Gergovie, Essalves, Magnindes, etc.; in Brittany: Kercaradec; in Cornwall: Gurnard's Head; in Ireland: Carrigillihy, Portadoon, Dun Aeongusa, Dun Cathair, Dun Eochla, Dun Eoghanachta, Staigue, Grianan of Ailigh, etc.*

C1-C2. *Drystone wall forts with peripheral ranges. West Coast of Scotland: Ardifuar, Borgue of Castlehaven, Druim an Duin, Dun Ringill, Dun Grugaig (Skye); in Northern Scotland: Clickhimin fort. Internal ranges were probably also present in promontory forts like Nybster, Caithness.*

C3-C4. *Galleried Duns: Dun Grugaig in Glen Elg, etc. Clickhimin blockhouse.*

C5. *Brochs: Clickhimin, Dun Carloway, Gurness, Jarlshof, Midhowe, Mousa, etc.*

this settlement was long established before a Late Bronze-Age smith set up his workshop in one of the houses probably in the late seventh or sixth century B.C.

At both sites the oval cubicled houses were superseded by large round-houses with internal diameters of up to twenty-five feet built by new immigrants who introduced carinated pottery in an Iron-Age A tradition.[15]

The next phase, missing at Jarlshof, is the most important one from the archaeological point of view at Clickhimin. It reflects the rising tide of Iron-Age penetration of the northern mainland and islands in the appearance of well organised bands capable of building sophisticated defence works. This colonisation was a northern extension of the widespread movements of Celtic immigrants into south-west Britain and Ireland from western Gaul and adjacent territories on the Continent during the fourth to second centuries B.C. At Clickhimin the newcomers built a fort on the tidal island. This comprised two major structures: an encircling fort wall ten to twelve feet thick round the shore of the islet with a gateway to the south facing the sandy isthmus; secondly, a blockhouse within this gateway. It enclosed the older round-house which was probably retained as an assembly or feasting hall.

The fort belongs to one of three main categories of Iron-Age fortification classified on rampart construction (fig. 2); all are drystone-built. The class (c), to which Clickhimin conforms, comprises forts in which the rampart is constructed as a simple rubble core wall with stone facing; the second category (B), known in Ireland and Cornwall, consisted of a series of casement walls (*murus duplex*) built to ascending heights giving a stepped appearance in section with the highest casement on the outside supporting the palisade or breastwork and rampart walk. The third category (A), includes drystone (or earth core) ramparts embodying timberlacing of the so-called Preist type, particularly characteristic of Iron-Age A defences in southern Britain and of the forts of Central Scotland.[16] All three techniques were introduced from the Continent where they had a wide distribution.

Large-scale excavation revealed for the first time the internal arrangement of such a fort (fig. 3). This included ranges of half-timbered storeyed buildings along the inner face of the fort wall and behind the blockhouse. At ground level the floors were of beaten earth or natural gravel with sporadic paving and cobbling. The ranges themselves were supported by upright posts and partition walling which carried wooden floors anchored at the rampart wall face or blockhouse wall on scarcement ledges.

The post-holes along the inner facade were well preserved. Measurements between these and the wall face as well as between each other allowed lengths of frontal beams, joists and partition walls to be calculated. Animal manure and winter bedding of peat-mould used in the stalls showed that part, at least, of the ground floor was given over to the hous-

Fig. 3. Reconstruction of Clickhimin fort showing drystone fort wall and blockhouse with storeyed timber ranges attached. The fort enclosure contains the remains of the Late Bronze-Age farmstead. The earlier Iron-Age roundhouse was retained (right centre) by the fort dwellers.

ing of cattle in the winter months. The first floor must have been devoted to storage as well as to living and sleeping quarters.

Hitherto our knowledge of the principles governing Iron-Age defences has been largely confined to *external factors*. A fort wall has been expected to perform two functions. First, it had to provide a screen or protective barrier against attack in the form of a wall with a vertical or near vertical face; second, it provided a defence platform comprising breastwork and wall-walk (fig. 2, A, B, C).

At Clickhimin, and other forts in the north, a second set of factors—
the internal or domestic—can now be defined. These factors, or pressures,
affect the inner half or face of the fort wall. The primary need was for a
vertical extension above wall-walk level in order to provide a casement
serving as the main rear wall of storeyed buildings (Fig. 2, c1-c4).

The floor in a storeyed range as at Clickhimin could be supported
by a ledge or scarcement course at wall-walk height, the roof being
anchored to the casement wall seven to nine feet above this level (fig. 2,
c1-c2). Access to the wall-walk or parapet-walk between the breastwork
and the casement could be obtained by stairs or by doorways leading
from the principal rooms at first-floor level.

In the next stage of development, governed by the need for two-
storeyed ranges inside the fort, the rear casement achieved a further
elevation (fig. 2, c3-c4). To keep pace with this internal expansion the
outer, defensive, element of the wall was carried up to provide a breastwork and wall-walk at second-floor level by hollow-wall construction and
slab-bonding. The second stage in fortification technique has been
achieved equivalent to that of the galleried duns or forts on the west
coast. Here the best preserved example is Dun Grugaig in Glen Elg with
an internal scarcement for a second-storey floor at fourteen feet above
ground level.[17] As we shall see later (p. 123) this stage was also present
at Clickhimin.

The interior wall faces of such forts, whether supporting single or
double storeyed ranges have acquired scarcements, doorways and aum-
bries above ground-floor level. It is precisely these features that we find
in a whole range of forts and duns down the west coast of Scotland as far
south as Galloway.[18] In many, features, which have not survived at Clickhimin, are excellently preserved such as the casement doorways leading
from the first floor of the timber ranges on to the parapet walks at Dun
Ringill[19] and Dun Grugaig[20] in Skye (fig. 4).

The question arises as to whether this development was peculiar to
Iron-Age fortifications along our northern and western coasts. There is
some evidence to suggest that interior wall ranges were also common
inside the timber-laced forts of central Scotland. The evidence is limited
at present and stems from the few scientifically explored vitrified examples. A convenient summary of the evidence is contained in Mrs
Cotton's survey:[21]

In the vitrified forts that have been scientifically excavated (Dun
Troon, Finavon, and Rahoy) a fierce conflagration within the fort
was attested by traces on the subsoil and by an astonishing number
of carbonised logs lying under the debris of the ramparts. At Finavon the charred timbers lay upon and above the hearths and floors

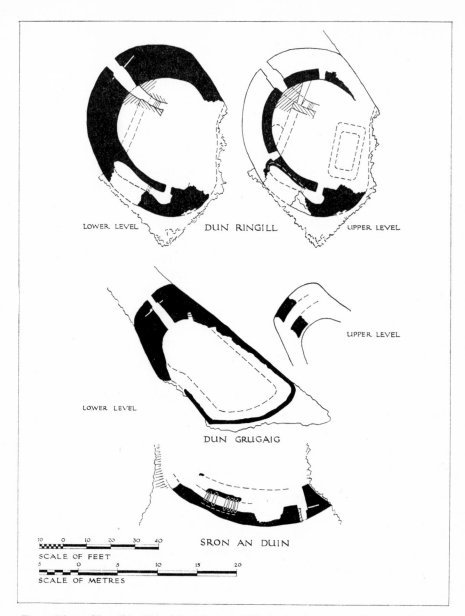

LOWER LEVEL   DUN RINGILL   UPPER LEVEL

UPPER LEVEL

LOWER LEVEL

DUN GRUGAIG

SRON AN DUIN

SCALE OF FEET

SCALE OF METRES

Fig. 4. Plans of Dun Ringill and Dun Grugaig (Skye), showing inner casement and doors at first-floor level which led from timber ranges to parapet walks, and of Sron an Duin, Barra Head.

of houses under the shelter of the north rampart; at Rahoy they lay upon the rock floor round Hearth 2.

If wall ranges were a feature of the timber-laced forts then the deliberate firing of these domestic structures under enemy attack may well have caused the timber-lacing to ignite and have reduced the walls to their vitrified state. Obviously only further excavation can clarify this point but it is certainly one to be borne in mind in the further examination of vitrified forts.

The most interesting implications arise, however, when we turn to Ireland and compare the internal layout of the Clickhimin type of fort with the 'duns' described in early Irish literature. One of the most puzzling anomalies of the Irish epics has been the fact that although the life portrayed is extremely archaic—the heroes, like Cuchulainn, are chariot-riding Celts practising head-hunting and undergoing tribal initiation rites similar to the *crypteia* and other customs described by early classical authors—the forts and 'palaces' they inhabit have been regarded since Petrie's day as belonging to a much later period.[22] If, however, we compare closely the descriptions with the present type of fort many of the sophisticated details fall into place and it would appear that, behind later accretions, a genuine tradition is preserved of the Iron-Age forts erected at the beginning of our era and probably already in use during the preceding centuries. The same phenomenon is seen in the memories of Mycenean palaces preserved down to the time of Homer in Greece.

When the arrangement of a fort with internal wall ranges is studied in conjunction with the texts a close identity becomes apparent. Within the central area enclosed by the fort wall one or more large communal or tribal houses can be discerned. The House of the Red Branch at Tara, for instance, housed the heads of vanquished enemies and served for assemblies and feasts. It was to such a 'hall' at Dun Rudraige that Bricriu invited the champions of Ireland to contend for the hero's portion.[23] He was not permitted to be present at the feast and retired to his 'grianan' or balcony.[24] This was not a kind of minstrels' gallery inside the hall as has been commonly supposed, but a feature of the chieftain's own house in the forepart of the court[25] in close proximity to the gateway. He spoke to one of the queens, Fedelm Nóichride, from this grianan on her way from the feasting hall to the gateway.[26] Later, when Cuchulainn in his rage pulled the hall into the ground, the whole dun shook, the house collapsed forward and Bricriu and his wife fell from their grianan into the filth of the courtyard.[27] The word *ocuid* means literally 'filth, muck' and not fosse as so often mistranslated. The stage directions, therefore, are compatible with a storeyed house or range along the inner face of the fort wall.

Pl. 3a (above) Clickhimin broch showing fort entrance, blockhouse and broch tower;
b (below) Clickhimin blockhouse inside fort entrance with inner ringwork surmounted by
broch (extreme left). Rear face scarcement and doorway at first-floor level.
(both Crown Copyright)

inches

Pl. 4 Fluted rim ware from Clickhimin. Sherds from cooking pots with everted rims heavily fluted or grooved. (Crown Copyright)

In another part of the tale we are told how the heroes and their
retainers are housed according to rank round the courtyard both at Dun
Rudraige[28] and at Cruachan[29]—heralds summoning them to the feasting-
hall.[30] Reference is also made to the separation of the men's and women's
quarters the latter being situated round the inner portion of the courtyard, the former in the forepart.[31] This appears to be a very early feature
of tribal society.

In the story of *The Burning of Da Derga's Hostel* the heroes and
champions are similarly housed around the central court as described by
the spy Ingcel. The facades of the buildings are frequently said to have
had carved wooden lintels and uprights[32]—quite feasible at this early
date from what we know of Celtic art and sculpture. Similarly, references
to many door openings have been regarded as archaeologically improb-
able, if not impossible, in a small dun or fort. But the references can be
applied to the doors leading from the first or second floor of a wall range
on to the wall walk. We are even told that they were constructed of
wicker hurdling and that as a rule they were closed to windward. Da
Derga's Hostel is described as follows:

> The chief one is Da Derga. 'Tis by him that the hostel was built,
> and since it was built its doors have never been shut save on the
> side to which the wind blows—the opening is closed against it—
> and since he began housekeeping his cauldron was never taken from
> the fire, but it has been boiling food for the men of Erin.
>
> There are seven doors into the house, and seven rooms between
> every two doorways; but there is only one doorway covering; and
> that covering is turned to every doorway to which the wind blows.[33]

Similarly references to beds between such doors become more readily
understandable in the light of storeyed ranges with living and sleeping
quarters at first-floor level or above. Mac Datho's dun for instance had
'seven doors in it, and fifty beds between each two doors'.[34] Obviously,
the numbers bear little relation to the truth. They belong to narrative
formulae so common in epic literature, but at least it may be claimed
they reflect a tradition based on the memory of buildings with a multiplicity of doors, rooms and couches which in themselves mirrored the
social status and wealth of their owners.

The storeyed nature of these ranges is not only recalled by the many
instances in which the women of the sagas climbed to their 'grianan' to
watch events in the courtyard and beyond the encircling wall of the dun,
but also by the vivid account given in *The Intoxication of the Ulstermen*[35]
of the firing under enemy attack of such structures:

> And the fire was lit from above and below in the house, until the
> heat from the fire came through the house from below. Then the

IANB I

hosts shouted loudly about the house so that the Ulstermen were silent, speechless, until Bricriu said 'What, O Ulstermen, is the great heat that seizes our feet? But it is fitter that I should know than any other person. It seems to me they are burning us from below, and from above; and the house is closed fast.'

That the ranges were not continuous round the inside of the dun but spaced irregularly as at Clickhimin is evident from such incidents as that described in the tale of *Diarmuid and Grainne*[36] in the Fenian cycle. In this episode the heroine escapes from Teamhair by leaving the grianan of her house through a doorway leading onto the rampart walk and then by climbing down the wall. Diarmuid, prevented from so doing by the rules of warrior conduct, had to leap the wall by vaulting on his spear shafts:

Diarmuid said 'This night Finn is in Teamhair and it is he himself is the keeper of the gates. And as that is so we cannot leave.' Grainne replied 'There is a side door of escape from my grianan and we will go out by it.' But Diarmuid said 'It is a thing I will never do, to go out by any side door of escape at all.' 'That may be so' said Grainne, 'but I have heard it said that any fighting man has leave to pass over the walls of any dun and of any strong place at all by the shafts of his spear. And I will go out through the door and let you follow me like that.' . . . And he went out then to the wall of the dun and he put the shafts of his two spears under him, and he rose with a light leap and he came down on the grassy earth and Grainne met him there.

In Ireland the internal perimeter arrangement may have been common to a wide range of forts as tradition implies, including the 'murus duplex' or stepped rampart forts of the south and west. Originally, as its Continental distribution suggests, this type of construction appears to have been devised to offset outward and downward thrust in defensive walls built in mountainous terrain.[37] But one, at least, of the 'steps' may correspond with floor levels inside individual timber ranges. The presence of such buildings particularly behind and over the main entrances is further suggested by the arrangement of tiered staircases leading from one level to the next. Early examples of this type of fort have been discovered on the coast of Cork,[38] in Cornwall,[39] and in Brittany.[40] At Kercaradec large post-holes were found between the outer and middle 'steps' indicating the presence of a timber wall corresponding to the stone casements in our northern forts.

Elsewhere in Britain the same peripheral arrangement of compartments or houses has been recognised in the Early Iron-Age A farmstead at West Harling in Norfolk[41] and is well known in the Cornish Iron-Age fort of Chun Castle.[42] The social arrangement reflected appears to be early and particularly associated with the Late Urnfield-Hallstatt-Iron-Age A peoples. Later on the Continent and in south-east Britain the small clan organisation appears to have been absorbed into the larger tribal groups capable of building oppida and hill-forts of much greater size and complexity in which the individual dwellings were spaced throughout the enclosures. Only in the extreme west and north did the earlier form of social organisation persist and flourish in conditions that were peculiarly favourable to clan society.

We may now consider the blockhouse set within the fort gateway at Clickhimin. It measures 42 feet in length and still stands to a height of 13 feet, only a proportion of its original elevation (pl. 3). The surviving details, however, are sufficient to show that it conformed to the building practices already described and that it was, in effect, a segment of a galleried fort wall conceived as a separate unit (see fig. 3, C3-C4), providing a wall walk and breastwork at second-floor level overlooking the fort gateway, while supporting a timber framed house at the rear. A partially paved floor extended backwards here for over 10 feet below later structures to give the approximate width of the dwelling.

The blockhouse was erected at the same time as the encircling fort wall. It may have been the intention to wed the two originally, but the plan was changed to the present layout. This duality in construction is apparent in other Shetland forts at the Loch of Huxter[43] and at the Ness of Burgi.[44] The Clickhimin blockhouse is built on an arc and though its maximum length is 42 feet the rear wall face is 34 feet at base. Allowing for the contracting batter at either end and taking into account the short length of the scarcement course which supported the first floor of the timber framed house the latter could not have exceeded 26 to 27 feet in length. At Huxter the blockhouse is 40 feet in length, but the encircling wall is attached at one end to the rear face, and again allowing for terminal batter, the dwelling behind could not have measured more than 30 feet; at the Ness of Burgi, a much larger structure measuring over 75 feet (it is incompletely preserved) in length, two ranges may have been accommodated one on either side of the entrance. That to the north on the complete side could not have exceeded 30 feet allowing for the contraction of terminal batter; that on the south side is unlikely to have exceeded 35 to 37 feet owing to the steep fall of the ground to the cliff edge. In all cases the blockhouses are the principal or most important structures associated with the encircling or promontory defences.

If we turn to the earliest Celtic laws in Ireland we find a possible explanation not only for the dual construction of these gate—or block—houses but also for their size.[45] A local chieftain (a *Flaith Bachald*) we are told 'is not entitled to have his dun built for him but only his house'. It would appear therefore that the erection of a fort or dun wall was a communal effort possibly already supervised, as Irish tradition suggests, by professional builders, the *Rath-Bhuidhe* (those who built the *Rath*, *Dun* and *Lis* formed of earth) and the *Caisleoir* who supervised the erection of the *Caiseal*, the *Cathair* and the *Dun* when it was constructed of stone.[46] It is apparent, for instance, that the Shetland blockhouses were built to well-conceived specifications which were even more rigorously observed by the later builders who constructed the broch towers throughout this northern province.

Some of the specifications, particularly those relating to the size of the houses were determined on social grounds. Thus, we find among the Irish Celts that the nobility and freeholders the *Flaiths* and the *Bo-Aires* were allocated houses of specified dimensions according to their social status.[47] The *Aire Desa*, the lowest grade of Flaiths or Aire, were entitled to a house of 27 feet; a leading Aire, *Aire Tuisi* had a house of 29 feet; the *Aire Forgaill*, next in rank after the king or his Tanist one of 30 feet; while the king himself occupied a house of 'seven feet and 30'. One of the most important functionaries among the Bo-Aires was the *mruigfer* who acted as judge or magistrate in tribal and family disputes. In virtue of his office he enjoyed the privilege of having a dun or wall and fosse about his dwelling, the house being one of 27 feet.

It was at his residence that the election of the King or *Righ Tuatha* took place, a ceremony which involved the use of a coronation stone (*leac-na-righ*) often bearing foot impressions in which the initiate stood to take the oath of kingship. This form of coronation ceremony survived in Ireland and the Western Isles down to the sixteenth century and coronation stones with foot impressions are recorded from both countries.[48] It is particularly interesting that just such a stone is found at Clickhimin built into the later causeway joining the islet site with the mainland. This association is secondary, the stone being used as a paving stone long after its original purpose was forgotten. It seems reasonable to suggest, in the absence of any such stones in wheel-house and broch contexts, that it was originally associated with the Iron-Age dun or fort on the islet. If the house measurements contained in the early Irish laws refer to length rather than diameter, that is to rectangular houses such as the individual units in peripheral ranges inside the duns rather than round huts, then an extraordinarily close agreement is found between those of the Bo-Aire class and the Clickhimin blockhouse range, which, we have shown, was approximately 27 feet in length. The presence of the foot-imprinted stone would seem to indicate that Clickhimin, if not the seat of a ruling Celtic family, was the residence of a local chieftain whose duties were similar to those of the later *mruigfer* and *rechtaire* described in Ireland.

There can be little doubt that the fort-builders were of Celtic stock. At Clickhimin they introduced ceramic styles which can be paralleled on sites in south-west Britain. Their pottery, for instance, included cooking-vessels with everted fluted rims, a fashion which was widespread in British south-west Iron-Age cultures and can be traced to north-west France[49] where it may ultimately be derived from the earlier Late Bronze-Age/Hallstatt wares of central and southern Gaul.[50] Even in our northern province the fluting of rims attained a widespread popularity which appears to have lasted for some considerable time (pl. 4). It was a common device at Clickhimin not only in the fort period but also during the succeeding broch and early wheel-house occupations. Fluted rims are recorded from other Shetland sites, Mousa,[51] Jarlshof,[52] Sae Breck,[53] and Olnesfirth[54] as well as in Orkney[55] and the Western Isles in early wheel-house contexts.[56] Another ornamental device which had a similar distribution at this time was a cordon or band of clay, slashed diagonally, applied on or just below the neck of such vessels. At Kercaradec in Brittany and at Chun in Cornwall, wares exhibiting these features are associated with a stepped rampart fort and a peripheral range fort respectively. The northern movement which brought the fort-builders to Shetland would appear to be a parallel, possibly related, movement to that which introduced the stepped rampart forts to Ireland. Certainly, as the name *Orcas* for the Orkneys already current in the first century B.C., and possibly much earlier, suggests, the Celtic element in the far north was an influential one. Other philological evidence in northern Scotland as Jackson shows appears to indicate that certain elements were Gallo-Brittonic speaking, some tribal names showing closer Gaulish than British connections.[57]

According to O'Rahilly a similar Gallo-Brittonic element is present in the early Iron-Age population of Ireland, particularly among the Ivernic tribes (the Firbolg) who are traditionally associated with the stepped rampart forts of southern and western Ireland.[58] Periods of folk migration often give rise to epic tales and the same scholar would relate three invasion stories (including the *Burning of Da Derga's Hostel* already quoted) to the arrival of the later Domnain-Galioin-Lagin in the third or second century B.C. The tribal name Domnain is identical with that of the Dumnonii or Damnonii of Cornwall, Devon and of south-west Scotland and its distribution in these areas round the Irish Sea may well reflect a northern maritime movement from the Continent at this period. The tales are concerned with two hero founders of the Laginian tribes notably Labraid Loingseach and Galioin who are reputed to have come from Armorica (Brittany).[59] Labraid is also represented as attacking strongholds of the Fomori on the west coast of Scotland as far north as Orkney.[60] It may be significant that descendants of Galioin are mentioned in traditional sources as the founders of the Picts in Orkney from whence they extended their power over the north mainland. In view of the colonies of fort-builders now defined by archaeology it is possible that these traditions contain at least an element of historical truth.

Towards the end of the fort period at Clickhimin the islet underwent severe flooding and an inner ring-wall enclosing the crest was under construction when new, but related, immigrants arrived—broch-builders from Orkney. It is important that the features common to fort and broch should be clearly defined in order to assess more readily the additional and specialised development which led to broch architecture. It is evident (fig. 2, c5) that the broch incorporates in a compact plan all the structural devices and principles of the earlier forts including an internal timber-frame range. At Clickhimin the circle of post-holes for the wooden uprights was recovered as at Dun Troddan.[61] The principal differences between the forts and the towers are the latter's more compact plan and additional height of 20 to 30 feet above second-floor level, a defensive rather than a domestic requirement.

The compact plan is already present in the smaller duns, but the strictly circular form is that universally adopted by the tower-builders. It is the ideal where defence is required by a small community engaged in colonisation or the utilisation of open land. Brochs do take advantage of rocky headlands, islets and earlier defence systems, but the majority occur in open tracts in Orkney and the river valleys of Caithness where the economic advantages of working arable soils outweighed the lack of topographical defence. Like the peel towers and Scottish tower-houses of later times the broch could stand alone.

The additional height is important. Though the hollow-wall or inner and outer casement construction embodies the principles already enumerated this high elevation could not have been readily achieved in the first place without abundant supplies of good building-stone. The distribution of the towers and geology—the Orkney and Caithness Old Red Sandstone Flags—suggest that specialisation first took place in one or other of these regions, traditional evidence giving preference to the Orkney Islands. If any reliance can be placed on the tradition that a treaty was concluded between the Roman fleet and the Orkney chieftains in 43 A.D., for instance, the islands would appear to have been the centre of political power.

The need for this defence in height must bear a close relationship to warfare at the time. It is perhaps significant that while in the far north additional protection was obtained in height, in southern Britain greater security was achieved by defence in depth—in the provision of multiple ramparts and ditches. In this respect insufficient attention may have been paid to a particular arm—the use of fire javelins and slings in Iron-Age warfare. Caesar described the devastation caused by such weapons in Gaul.[62] Irish sources refer to the reduction by fire of strongholds of the Fomori, possibly on the west coast of Scotland, and in the Ultonian cycle many strongholds are described as being destroyed by fire. In central and western Scotland there is the extremely significant evidence of the vitrified forts, many examples extending in a 'frontier' zone down the Great Glen and the west coast.

Fire javelins or spears must have been made of readily expendable materials. It is significant that we have in the castle area of the north hollow sheepbone darts or javelin points,[63] common enough in the south, but obviously capable of military application as is shown by their occurrence in the rich warrior graves of East Yorkshire together with La Tène shields, spears and swords.[64] Viewed against such a background, the broch appears as the logical successor to the forts. With its high-level firing platform at wall-top height ordinary slingers could make approach difficult, while the towering wall face afforded protection to the domestic timber structures inside the court from the fire slings and javelins of attacking forces.

At Clickhimin, as on other sites, the need for more specialised defence passed away. In the succeeding period the height of the tower was deliberately reduced, the dismantled stone being stacked for a time outside the tower entrance, where a layer of builder's rubble accumulated, and was then incorporated in the fabric of the wheel-house inside the broch. In the peat-ash overlying the builder's rubble a fragment of Roman glass of late first- or early second-century date suggests that the change in the political climate was already advanced by the middle of the second century A.D. The wheel-house period, as at Jarlshof and elsewhere, was of long duration and in the mounting refuse round the tower small outbuildings and huts were erected at various intervals of time. With the silting up of the narrow strait a stone causeway was built from the mainland to the islet. Evidence suggests that occupation had ceased before the coming of the Vikings in the ninth century.

The events on these two sites have provided a fairly complete chronological sequence for the Iron Age in the Shetland Islands. Despite the remoteness of the islands the underlying pattern is familiar. It begins, as in the south, with the ever increasing penetration of Iron-Age colonists from the fifth or fourth centuries B.C. It culminates in a crescendo of fort and castle building in the last two centuries B.C. extending into the second century of our era. For the Atlantic Province, at least, we must modify our conception of the Highland Zone as a remote and backward area during the Iron Age where external influences were slowly assimilated. Celtic colonists, as in the south, introduced a complex clan society and military organisation of great vitality, the latter being sufficiently strong to encourage the development of specialised broch defences. At last, after a century of speculation and research, we can see these towers as the final and finest expression of an evolutionary series of fortification techniques.

With the advent of Roman power and the subsequent preoccupation of the mainland confederacies with the Romanised Province to the south, the far north it may be surmised was left to its own devices.[65] It lapsed into a cultural backwater, political power ebbing south to the mainland tribes known collectively as the Picts from the end of the third century. The area was only to enter the main stream of history again on the expansion of the Scandinavian peoples in the ninth and tenth centuries of our era.

Notes

1. J. Anderson, 'Notes on the Structure, Distribution and Contents of the Brochs', *PSAS* XII (1876-8), 314-55; *Scotland in Pagan Times: The Iron Age*, 1883.
2. J. Anderson, ibid. (1883), 243.
3. J. G. Callander and W. G. Grant, 'The Broch of Midhowe', *PSAS* LXVII, 444-516.
4. J. S. Richardson, *The Broch of Gurness* (H.M.S.O. 1948), pp. 1-8.
5. J. Anderson, 'Notices of Nine Brochs along the Caithness Coast', *PSAS* XXXV (1900-1), 112-48.
6. See V. G. Childe, *Prehistory of Scotland*, 202.
7. R.C.A.H.M. IX, p. xxxvi, fig. 6.
8. Sir Lindsay Scott, 'The Problem of the Brochs', *PPS* XIII (1947), 1, also 'Gallo-British Colonies: The Aisled Roundhouse Culture in the North', *PPS* XIV (1948), 46-125.
9. Sir Lindsay Scott, 'The Aisled Roundhouse Culture', ibid., 114.
10. J. R. C. Hamilton, *Excavations at Jarlshof* (1956).
11. J. R. C. Hamilton, ibid., 46-8.
12. J. R. C. Hamilton, *Excavations at Clickhimin, Shetland* (H.M.S.O., forthcoming).
13. C. S. T. Calder, 'Stone Age House Sites in Shetland', *PSAS* LXXXIX (1955-6), 340-97.

14. J. R. C. Hamilton, 'Brochs and Broch Builders', in F. T. Wainwright (ed.), *The Northern Isles*, 53-4.

15. J. R. C. Hamilton, *Excavations at Jarlshof, Shetland*, 39, figs. 18-20.

16. M. Aylwin Cotton, 'British Camps with Timber-laced Ramparts', *Arch. J* CXI (1954), 26-105.

17. L. Bogle, 'Prehistoric Structures in Glen Elg', *PSAS* XXIX, 180.

18. Conveniently described in V. G. Childe, *Prehistory of Scotland*, 197-202.

19. R.C.A.H.M. IX, no. 650.

20. R.C.A.H.M. IX, no. 651.

21. M. Aylwin Cotton, *Arch. J* CXI (1954), 100.

22. G. Petrie, 'On the History and Antiquities of Tara Hill', *TRIA* XVIII (1839), 197ff.

23. *Fled Bricrend*, trans. G. Henderson (Irish Text Society), Vol. 2 (1899), Ch. I, 1-4.

24. Ibid., II, 13.

25. Ibid., II, 12.

26. Ibid., III, 17.

27. Ibid., III, 25.

28. Ibid., II, 12.

29. Ibid., VIII, 54.

30. Ibid., X, 59-61.

31. Ibid., II, 12.

32. Ibid., VIII, 55: I.2.

33. *Togail Bruidne Da Derga*; see Stokes, *Rev. Celt.* XXII.

34. *Mucc Meic Da Tho*, para. 1; see *Rev. Celt.* XXI, 396ff.

35. R. Thurneysen, *Die Irische Helden- und Königsage* (Halle 1921), 473.

36. S. H. O'Grady, 'Pursuit of Diarmaid and Grainne'. *Transactions of the Ossianic Society* III.

37. See Déchelette, *Manuel d'Archéologie*, III (1927), 191, fig. 270.

38. M. J. O'Kelly, 'Three Promontory Forts in Co. Cork', *PRIA* 55 (1952-3), 25.

39. A. S. R. Gordon, 'The Excavation of Gurnard's Head', *Arch. J* XCVII (1940), 96-111.

40. Sir R. M. Wheeler and K. M. Richardson, *Hill Forts of Northern France* (1957), 54.

41. J. G. D. Clark and C. I. Fell, 'The Early Iron Age Site at Micklemoor Hill, West Harling', *PPS* XIX (1953), 1-40.

42. *Arch.* LXXVI, 205-39.

43. A. Mitchell, 'Notice of Buildings, Loch of Huxter', *PSAS* XV (1880-1), 303; R.C.A.H.M.(S.), no. 1316.

44. C. L. Mowbray, 'Excavations at the Ness of Burgi', *PSAS* LXX (1935-6), 381; R.C.A.H.M.(S.), no. 1154.

45. E. O'Curry, *The Manners and Customs of the Ancient Irish*, Vol. III, Part ii, 467ff.

46. A list of the Legendary builders of Duns and Raths is given in *The Book of Leinster*, fol. 27b.

47. See E. MacNeill, 'Ancient Irish Law', *PRIA* XXXVI, 265-316; also comments by D. A. Binchy, *Crith Gablach* (Dublin, 1941), 77ff.

48. See F. W. L. Thomas, 'Dunadd: the Place of Inauguration of the Dalriadic Kings', *PSAS* XIII, 28ff; T. J. Westropp, 'Magh Adhair, Co. Clare. The Place of Inauguration of the Diacassian Kings', *PRIA* IV (1896-8), 55ff.

49. R. E. Mortimer Wheeler and K. M. Richardson, *Hill Forts of Northern France* (1957), 59, fig. 12.

50. N. K. Sanders, *Bronze Age Cultures in France* (1957). See e.g. Yonne, fig. 49: Doubs and Jura, fig. 51; the Dordogne, fig. 67.

51. Nat. Mus. Ants., Ref. no. GA 1.121.

52. J. R. C. Hamilton, *Excavations at Jarlshof* (1956), p. 65, fig. 35, 3.

53. C. S. T. Calder, 'Report on the Partial Excavation of a Broch at Sae Breck, Shetland', Report on the pottery by J. R. C. Hamilton, *PSAS* LXXXVI, pp. 181ff.

54. Nat. Mus. Ants., no. L1948. 76 GE.57.

55. Broch of Ayre; Nat. Mus. Ants., L1948. 83; Okstrow: Nat. Mus. Ants., GD.47-48; Cairston: Nat. Mus. Ants., no. GA.298.

56. Clettreval: Lindsay Scott, *Gallo British Colonies*, fig. 5 type IB; Foshigarry: *PSAS* LXV, 300, fig. 25. Since the above was written, a pre-broch sequence similar to that established at Clickhimin has been confirmed in the Western Isles; see E. W. Mackie, 'Brochs and the Hebridean Iron Age', *Ant.* XXXIX (1965), 266-78, and *PPS* XXXI (1965), 93-146.

57. K. Jackson, 'The Pictish Language' in Wainwright (ed.), *The Problem of the Picts*, 138.

58. T. R. O'Rahilly, *Early Irish History and Mythology* (Dublin, 1947), 43-91.

59. Ibid., 99-140.

60. *Orgain Dinn Rig*. See H. M. Chadwick, *Early Scotland* (1949), 113.

61. A. O. Curle, 'The Broch of Dun Troddan', *PSAS* LV (1920-1), 83-94.

62. Caesar, *De Bello Gallico*, V, 43; VII, 24; VII, 25.

63. V. G. Childe, *Prehistory of Scotland*, 241.

64. See B.M. Guide, *Early Iron Age Antiquities* (1925), 113.

65. J. R. C. Hamilton, 'Brochs & Broch Builders', in F. T. Wainwright (ed.), *The Northern Isles* (1962), 89.

BIBLIOGRAPHY

A. L. F. RIVET

The system of abbreviations employed in the notes should enable the reader to follow up any particular reference without recourse to this bibliography. In view of this, rather than simply to list the works referred to it has seemed more useful to prepare a comprehensive (though still not exhaustive) bibliography of the Iron Age in Northern Britain and to include not only the works already cited but also a much wider selection, especially of excavation reports. The list is inevitably a long one, and to make it more easily usable it has been divided as follows:

1. *General.* This section includes works of general interest and importance, both books and papers in periodicals, whose scope extends beyond a single province. Some works concerned with Britain as a whole are included, but only those which have a northern application.

2. *Art, Metal-work etc.* Within its more limited terms of reference, this section follows the same general principles as section 1.

3. *Provincial.* Each of the North British Provinces is given its own section, and this in turn is subdivided into two parts:

(*a*) General, consisting for the most part of regional surveys including the volumes published by the Royal Commission on the Ancient and Historical Monuments of Scotland.

(*b*) Individual Sites. The majority of the references here, those indicated by an asterisk (*), are to excavation reports, but especially where no Commission volume has yet appeared some descriptions based on surveys without excavation are also included. In each case the type of site referred to is indicated in brackets.

In addition to the four Provinces with which this book is concerned, a few references are included to surveys and sites in the Pennine and Eastern Provinces which lie to the south. This section does not, of course, pretend to be comprehensive and is restricted to matter which is of primary interest to the student of the northern Provinces.

It is realised that not all the classifications will meet with universal agreement. Opinions differ, for example, on where the line should be drawn between Brochs and Galleried Duns on the one hand and between Duns and Forts on the other, and no distinction is made here between Wheel-houses proper and Aisled Round-houses.

GENERAL

ANDERSON, James, 'An Account of the Ancient Monuments and Fortifications in the Highlands of Scotland', *Arch.* V (1779), 87-99.

— 'A Further Description of Ancient Fortifications in the North of Scotland', *Arch.* VI (1782), 87-99.

ANDERSON, Joseph, *Scotland in Pagan Times: The Iron Age*, Rhind Lectures, 1881 (Edinburgh, 1883).

CHILDE, V. G., *Prehistoric Communities of the British Isles*, 2nd edn. (London, 1947).

— *The Prehistory of Scotland* (London, 1935).

— *Scotland before the Scots* (London, 1946).

— and SIMPSON, W. D., *Ancient Monuments, Scotland* (Vol. VI of *Illustrated Guide to Ancient Monuments*) (Edinburgh, 1961).

— and THORNEYCROFT, W., 'The Experimental Production of the Phenomena Distinctive of Vitrified Forts', *PSAS* LXXII (1937-8), 44-55.

CHRISTISON, D., *Early Fortifications in Scotland*, Rhind Lectures, 1894 (Edinburgh, 1898).

COTTON, M. A., 'British Camps with Timber-laced Ramparts', *Arch. J* CXI (1955), 26-105.

CURLE, J., *A Roman Frontier Post and its People: The Fort of Newstead* (Glasgow, 1911).

FEACHEM, R. W., *A Guide to Prehistoric Scotland* (London, 1963).

— 'Unenclosed Platform Settlements', *PSAS* XCIV (1960-1), 79-85.

— *The North Britons* (London, 1966).

FOX, C., *The Personality of Britain*, 4th edn. (Cardiff, 1947).

FRERE, S. S. (ed.), *Problems of the Iron Age in Southern Britain*, University of London Institute of Archaeology Occasional Paper No. 11 (London, n.d. [1961]).

GRAHAM, A., 'Some Observations on the Brochs', *PSAS* LXXXI (1946-7), 48-98.

HAMILTON, J. R. C., *Excavations at Jarlshof, Shetland* (Edinburgh, 1956).

— *Excavations at Clickhimin, Shetland* (Edinburgh, forthcoming).

HARDEN, D. B. (ed.), *Dark Age Britain* (London, 1956).

HAWKES, C. F. C., 'The ABC of the British Iron Age', *Ant.* XXXIII (1959), 170-82 (and in *Problems of the Iron Age in S. Britain*).

HAWKES, J. and C., *Prehistoric Britain*, revised edn. (Harmondsworth, 1958).

HIBBERT, S., 'Observations on the Theories which have been proposed to explain the Vitrified Forts of Scotland, with Collections relative to Vitrified Sites', *Arch. Scot.* IV (1857), 160-201 and 280-97.

HONEYMAN, J., 'Remarks on the Construction of Vitrified Forts', *T Glasgow AS* (os) II (1883), 29-34.

JACKSON, K., *Language and History in Early Britain* (Edinburgh, 1953).

— 'The Britons in Southern Scotland', *Ant.* XXIX (1955), 77-88.

LETHBRIDGE, T. C., 'Excavations at Kilpheder, South Uist, and the Problem of Brochs and Wheel-houses', *PPS* XVIII (1952), 176-93.

M'HARDY, A., 'On Vitrified Forts, with Results of Experiments as to the Probable Manner in which their Vitrification may have been produced', *PSAS* XL (1905-6), 136-50.

MACKIE, E. W., 'The Origin and Development of the Broch and Wheelhouse Building Cultures of the Scottish Iron Age', *PPS* XXXI (1965), 93-146.

MACLAGAN, C., *The Hill Forts, Stone Circles and other Structural Remains of Ancient Scotland* (Edinburgh, 1875).

MACRITCHIE, D., 'Earth-houses and their Occupants', *PSAS* LI (1916-17), 178-98.

MUNRO, R., *Ancient Scottish Lake Dwellings* (Edinburgh, 1882).

— *The Lake Dwellings of Europe* (London, 1890).

— *Prehistoric Scotland* (London, 1899).

PIGGOTT, S., *British Prehistory* (Oxford, 1949).

— (ed.), *The Prehistoric Peoples of Scotland* (London, 1962).

RICHMOND, I. A., *Roman Britain*, 2nd edn. (Harmondsworth, 1963).

— (ed.), *Roman and Native in North Britain* (Edinburgh, 1958).

SALWAY, P., *The Frontier People of Roman Britain* (Cambridge, 1965).

SCOTT, L., 'Gallo-British Colonies. The Aisled Round-house Culture in the North', *PPS* XIV (1948), 46-125.

— 'The Colonisation of Scotland in the Second Millennium B.C.', *PPS* XVII (1951), 16-82.

— 'The Problem of the Brochs', *PPS* XIII (1947), 1-36.

STEER, K. A., 'The Identification of Palisaded Enclosures from Surface Indications', *PSAS* LXXXIII (1948-9), 64-7.

STEVENSON, R. B. K., 'The Nuclear Fort of Dalmahoy, Midlothian, and other Dark Age Capitals (Dunadd, Dundurn, Ruberslaw)', *PSAS* LXXXIII (1948-9), 186-97.

WAINWRIGHT, F. T., *The Souterrains of Southern Pictland* (London, 1963).

— (ed.), *The Problem of the Picts* (Edinburgh, 1956).

WATSON, W. J., *History of the Celtic Place-names of Scotland* (Edinburgh, 1926).

WILLIAMS, John, *An Account of Some Remarkable Ancient Ruins, Lately Discovered in the Highlands and Northern Parts of Scotland* (Edinburgh, 1777).

WILSON, D., *The Archaeology and Prehistoric Annals of Scotland* (Edinburgh, 1857); 2nd edn., 2 vols (London and Cambridge, 1863).

YOUNG, A., 'Brochs and Duns', *PSAS* XCV (1961-2), 171-98.

ART, METAL-WORK, ETC.

ANDERSON, J., 'Notice of a Bronze Bucket-shaped Vessel or Caldron, exhibited by H. D. Erskine, Esq., of Cardross', *PSAS* XXII (1887-8), 36-42.

— 'Notice of a Bronze Caldron found with several small Kegs of Butter in a Moss near Kyleakin, Skye; with Notes of other Caldrons of Bronze found in Scotland', *PSAS* XIX (1884-5), 309-15 (includes Kincardine Moss).

— 'Note on a Late Celtic Armlet of Bronze (Bunrannoch) now presented to the National Museum: with Notes on the Identification of two other Late Celtic Armlets in the Museum (Pitalpin & Stitchell), and on a Massive Bronze Armlet recently found in Sutherlandshire (Rogart)', *PSAS* XXXVIII (1903-4), 460-7.

— 'Notes on a Romano-British Hoard of Bronze Vessels & Personal Ornaments found in a Moss on Lamberton Moor, Berwickshire', *PSAS* XXXIX (1905-6), 367-76.

— 'Notes on the Evidence of Spinning and Weaving in the Brochs or Pictish Towers supplied by the Stone Whorls and the Long-handled "Broch Combs" found in them', *PSAS* IX (1871-2), 548-61.

ATKINSON, R. J. C., and PIGGOTT, S., 'The Torrs Chamfrein', *Arch.* XCVI (1955), 197-235.

BRAILSFORD, J. W., *Later Prehistoric Antiquities of the British Isles*, B.M. Guide (London, 1953).

BURLEY, E., 'A Catalogue and Survey of the Metal-Work from Traprain Law', *PSAS* LXXXIX (1955-6), 118-226.

CALLANDER, J. G., 'An Early Iron Age Hoard from Crichie, near Inverurie', *PSAS* LXI (1926-7), 243-6.

— 'Three Stone Cups found in a Cairn in Aberdeenshire (with discussion of Stone Cups in general)', *PSAS* L (1915-16), 145-50.

COLES, J. M., 'Scottish Late Bronze Age Metalwork', *PSAS* XCIII (1959-60), 16-134.

— 'Scottish Swans-Neck Sunflower Pins', *PSAS* XCII (1958-9), 1-9.

COLLINGWOOD, R. G., 'Romano-Celtic Art in Northumbria', *Arch.* LXXX (1930), 37-58.

CRAW, J. H., 'On Two Bronze Spoons from an Early Iron Age Grave near Burnmouth, Berwickshire', *PSAS* LVIII (1923-4), 143-59.

CURLE, J., 'An Enamelled Bronze Belt-plate and Dress Fastener from Drumashie, Dores, Inverness-shire', *PSAS* LVIII (1923-4), 11-12.

— 'Objects of Roman and Provincial Roman Origin found on Sites in Scotland not definitely associated with Roman Constructions', *PSAS* LXVI (1931-2), 277-397.

FEACHEM, R. W., 'Dragonesque Fibulae, *Ant. J* XXXI (1951), 32-44.

— 'The "Cairnmuir" Hoard from Netherurd, Peeblesshire', *PSAS* XCI (1957-8), 112-16.

FOWLER, E., 'The Origins and Development of the Penannular Brooch in Europe', *PPS* XXVI (1960), 149-77.

FOX, C., *Pattern and Purpose: Early Celtic Art in Britain* (Cardiff, 1958).

HAWKES, C. F. C., 'Bronze-Workers, Cauldrons and Bucket-Animals in Iron Age and Roman Britain', in Grimes, W. F. (ed.), *Aspects of Archaeology in Britain and Beyond* (London, 1951).

— and SMITH, M. A., 'On some Buckets and Cauldrons of the Bronze and Early Iron Ages: the Nannau, Whigsborough and Heathery Burn Bronze Buckets and the Colchester and London Cauldrons', *Ant. J* XXXVII (1957), 131-98.

JACOBSTHAL, P., *Early Celtic Art* (Oxford, 1944).

JOPE, E. M., 'Daggers of the Early Iron Age in Britain', *PPS* XXVII (1961), 307-43.

— 'The Beginnings of La Tène Ornamental Style in the British Isles', in Frere, S. S. (ed.), *Problems of the Iron Age in Southern Britain* (London, 1961).

KILBRIDE-JONES, H. E., 'An Aberdeenshire Iron Age Miscellany, (2) Bronze Terret from Rhynie, and Distribution of the Type', *PSAS* LXIX (1934-5), 448-54.

— 'Glass Armlets in Britain', *PSAS* LXXII (1937-8), 366-95.

— 'Scots Zoomorphic Penannular Brooches', *PSAS* LXX (1935-6), 124-38.

— 'The Evolution of Penannular Brooches with Zoomorphic Terminals in Great Britain and Ireland', *PRIA* XLIII (1935-7), 379-455.

LEEDS, E. T., *Celtic Ornament in the British Isles down to A.D. 700* (Oxford, 1933).

MACGREGOR, M., 'The Early Iron Age Metalwork Hoard from Stanwick, N.R. Yorks', *PPS* XXVIII (1962), 17-57.

MAXWELL, H. E., 'Notice of an Enamelled Bronze Harness Ornament, from Auchendolly, Stewartry of Kirkcudbright', *PSAS* XX (1885-6), 396-8.

PIGGOTT, S., 'Swords and Scabbards of the British Early Iron Age', *PPS* XVI (1950), 1-28.

— 'The Carnyx in Early Iron Age Britain', *Ant. J* XXXIX (1959), 19-32.

— 'Three Metal-work Hoards of the Roman Period from Southern Scotland (Carlingwark, Blackburn Mill, Eskford)', *PSAS* LXXXVII (1952-3), 1-50.

SMITH, J. A., 'Notice of a Massive Bronze "Late Celtic" Armlet and two small Objects of Bronze (horse-trappings) found with a Roman Bronze Patella, at Stanhope, Peeblesshire, in 1876; with an Account of other Bronze or Brass Armlets found in Scotland', *PSAS* XV (1880-1), 316-69.

— 'Notice of a Remarkable Bronze Ornament with Horns, found in Galloway, now at Abbotsford (the Torrs "Chamfrein"); also of a Bronze Ornament like a "Swine's Head", found in Banffshire (the Deskford Carnyx); with Notes on Bronze and Silver Ornaments in the Museum of the Society', *PSAS* VII (1867-8), 334-57.

SMITH, R. A., *Early Iron Age Antiquities*, B.M. Guide, 2nd edn. (London, 1925).

STEVENSON, R. B. K., 'Native Bangles and Roman Glass', *PSAS* LXXXVIII (1953-5), 208-21.

— 'Notes on Some Prehistoric Objects (incl. the Kelton bronze torc)', *PSAS* LXXXII (1947-8), 293-4.

— 'Pins and the Chronology of the Brochs', *PPS* XXI (1955), 282-94.

THOMAS, A. C., 'The Animal Art of the Scottish Iron Age and its Origins', *Arch. J* CXVIII (1961), 14-64.

TYLECOTE, R. F., *Metallurgy in Archaeology—A Prehistory of Metallurgy in the British Isles* (London, 1962).

WARD PERKINS, J. B., 'Iron Age Metal Horses' Bits of the British Isles', *PPS* V (1939), 173-92.

ATLANTIC PROVINCE

General

ANDERSON, J., 'Notice of the Excavation of the Brochs of Yarhouse, Brounaben, Bowermadden, Old Stirkoke, and Dunbeath, in Caithness, with Remarks on the Period of the Brochs: and an Appendix, containing a Collected List of the Brochs of Scotland, and early Notices of Many of them', *Arch. Scot.* V (1890), 131-98.

BEVERIDGE, E., *Coll and Tiree: their Prehistoric Forts and Ecclesiastical Antiquities; with notes of Ancient Remains in the Treshnish Isles* (Edinburgh, 1903).

— *North Uist: its Archaeology and Topography; with notes on the Early History of the Outer Hebrides* (Edinburgh, 1911).

BOGLE, L., 'Notes on some Prehistoric Structures in Glenelg and Kintail (Brochs)', *PSAS* XXIX (1894-5), 180-90.

CAMPBELL, M., and SANDEMAN, M., 'Mid-Argyll; an Archaeological Survey', *PSAS* XCV (1961-2), 1-125.

CHILDE, V. G., 'Notes on some Duns in Islay', *PSAS* LXIX (1934-5), 81-4.

CHRISTISON, D., 'The Duns and Forts of Lorne, Nether Lochaber and the Neighbourhood', *PSAS* XXIII (1888-9), 368-432.

— 'The Forts of Kilmartin, Kilmichael Glassary and North Knapdale, Argyle', *PSAS* XXXVIII (1903-4), 205-51.

DRYDEN, H., 'Notes of the Brochs or "Pictish Towers" of Mousa, Clickemin, &c. in Shetland, illustrative of part of the Series of Plans and Sections deposited in the Library of the Society', *Arch. Scot.* V (1890), 199-212.

HEWISON, J. K., 'On the Prehistoric Forts of the Island of Bute', *PSAS* XXVII (1892-3), 281-93.

ISLAY ARCHAEOLOGICAL SURVEY GROUP, *Preliminary Handbook to the Archaeology of Islay* (London, 1959); Additions, 1960; Bibliography, 1961.

JOASS, J. M., 'The Brochs or "Pictish Towers" of Cinn-Trolla, Carn-Liath, and Craig-Carril, in Sutherland, with Notes on other Northern Brochs', *Arch. Scot.* V (1890), 95-130.

JONES, J. D., and PIGGOTT, C. M., 'Brochs and Duns in Tiree', *PSAS* LXXXVI (1951-2), 196-8.

KEDDIE, W., 'On the Remains of a Vitrified Fort, or Site, in the Island of Cumbrae, with Notes on the Vitrified Forts of Berigonium, Glen Nevis, Craig Phadrick, Portencross, and Bute', *T Glasgow AS* (OS) I (1868), 236-55.

MACADAM, W. I., 'Notes on Ancient Structures in the Islands of Seil and Luing, and in the Garbh Island: with preliminary notice of the North Fort of Luing', *PSAS* XXX (1895-6), 23-9.

MACKIE, E. W., 'The Broch of Dun Mor Vaul, Tiree, and the Cultural Components of the Hebridean Iron Age', *Ant.* XXXIX (1965), 266-78.

PETRIE, G., 'Notice of the Brochs or Large Round Towers of Orkney, with Plans, Sections, and Drawings, and Tables of Measurements of Orkney and Shetland Brochs, *Arch. Scot.* V (1890), 71-94.

PIGGOTT, S. and C. M., 'Field-Work in Colonsay and Islay, 1944-45', *PSAS* LXXX (1945-6), 83-102.

R.C.A.H.M.(S), *Argyll*, forthcoming.
 Caithness (1911).
 Orkney and Shetland (1946).
 The Outer Hebrides, Skye and the Small Isles (1928).
 Sutherland (1911).

STOUT, E., 'Some Shetland Brochs and Standing Stones', *PSAS* XLVI (1911-12), 94-132.

THOMAS, F. W. L., 'On the Duns of the Outer Hebrides', *Arch. Scot.* V, (1890), 365-415.

— 'On the Primitive Dwellings and Hypogea of the Outer Hebrides', *PSAS* VII (1866-7), 153-95.

WAINWRIGHT, F. T. (ed.), *The Northern Isles* (Edinburgh, 1962).

Individual Sites

*a' Cheardach Mhor, Drimore, S. Uist (Wheel-house): Young, A., *PSAS* XCIII (1959-60), 135-73.

*Aignish, Lewis (Settlement): Curwen, E. C., *PSAS* LXXIII (1938-9), 55-7.

*An Caisteal, Mull (Fort): Fairhurst, H., *PSAS* XCV (1961-2), 199-207.

*An-Cnap, Arran (Fort): Noel Paton, V. A., *PSAS* LXII (1927-8), 239-41.

An Dun, Drienach, Strath Kanaird (Dun): Calder, C. S. T., and Steer, K. A., *PSAS* LXXXIII (1948-9), 76.

An Dun, Gairloch, Ross (Fort): Graham, A., *PSAS* LXXXIII (1948-9), 23-4.

*Ardifuar, Argyll (Galleried Dun): Christison, D., Anderson, J., and Ross, T. T., *PSAS* XXXIX (1904-5), 259-70.

*Ayre, Orkney (Broch): Sutherland Graeme, A., *PSAS* XLVIII (1913-14), 31-51.

IANB K

*Bac Mhic Connain, N. Uist (Wheel-house): Beveridge, E., and Callander, J. G., *PSAS* LXVI (1931-2), 42-66.

*Balevullin, Tiree (Dwelling Site): MacKie, E. W., *PSAS* XCVI (1962-3), 155-83.

Bard's Castle, Bundalloch, Ross (Fort): Graham, A., *PSAS* LXXXIII (1948-9), 22-3.

*Biggings, Harray, Orkney (Souterrain): Kirkness, W., *PSAS* LXIV (1929-30), 222-32.

*Brindister, Shetland (Broch): Goudie, G., *PSAS* XXIII (1888-9), 246-9.

*Burrian, N. Ronaldsay, Orkney (Broch): Traill, W., *Arch. Scot.* V (1890), 341-64.

*Burwick (Borwick), Sandwick, Orkney (Broch): Watt, W. G. T., *PSAS* XVI (1881-2), 442-50.

Caisteal Grugaig, Totaig, Ross (Broch): Graham, A., *PSAS* LXXXIII (1948-9), 14-19.

*Calf of Eday, Orkney (Wheel-house): Calder, C. S. T., *PSAS* LXXIII (1938-9), 167-84.

*Clachan Ard, Bute (Fort): Marshall, J. N., *PSAS* LXVIII (1933-4), 420-2, and *T Bute NHS* XI (1935), 80-3.

*Clumlie, Shetland (Broch): Goudie, G., *PSAS* XXIII (1888-9), 249-53.

*Clyne Milton, Sutherland (Souterrain): Serjeantson, R. J., *PSAS* LXIV (1929-30), 200-1.

*Dale, Harray, Orkney (Souterrain): Kirkness, W., *PSAS* LXII (1927-8), 155-61.

*Druim an Duin, Argyll (Dun): Christison, D., Anderson, J., and Ross, T., *PSAS* XXXIX (1904-5), 285-92.

Dunadd, Argyll (Fort): Thomas, F. W. L., *PSAS* XIII (1878-9), 28-47.

— *: Christison, D., Anderson, J., and Ross, T., *PSAS* XXXIX (1904-5), 292-322.

— *: Craw, J. H., *PSAS* LXIV (1929-30), 111-27.

*Dunagoil, Bute (Fort): Marshall, J. N., *T Bute NHS* VIII (1914-15), 42-9 and Mann, L., ibid., 68-86.

*Dun an Iardhard, Skye (Broch): Macleod, F. T., *PSAS* XLIX (1914-15), 57-70.

*Dunan na Nighean, Colonsay (Dun): Piggott, C. M., *PSAS* LXXXIII (1948-9), 232.

Dun an Ruigh Ruadh, Rhiroy, Ross (Broch): Calder, C. S. T., and Steer, K. A., *PSAS* LXXXIII (1948-9), 72-4.

*Dun Beag, Struan, Skye (Broch): Callander, J. G., *PSAS* LV (1920-1), 110-30.

*Dun Breac, Skipness, Argyll (Dun): Graham, A., *PSAS* XLIX (1914-15), 50-6.

Dun Canna, Ullapool, Ross (Fort): Calder, C. S. T., and Steer, K. A., *PSAS* LXXXIII (1948-9), 74-5.

*Dun Cuier, Barra (Galleried Dun): Young, A., *PSAS* LXXXIX (1955-6), 290-328.

*Dun Fheurain, Oban, Argyll (Midden at base of Dun): Anderson, J., *PSAS* XXIX (1894-5), 278-85.

Dun Grugaig, Glenelg, Inverness (Galleried Dun): Graham, A., *PSAS* LXXXIII (1948-9), 19-22.

Dun Lagaidh, Loch Broom, Ross (Fort and Broch): Calder, C. S. T., and Steer, K. A., *PSAS* LXXXIII (1948-9), 68-72.

*Dun Telve, Glenelg, Inverness (Broch): Curle, A. O., *PSAS* L (1915-16), 241-56.

*Dun Thomaidh, N. Uist (Galleried Dun): Beveridge, E., and Callander, J. G., *PSAS* LXV (1930-1), 317-57.

*Dun Troddan, Glenelg, Inverness (Broch): Curle, A. O., *PSAS* LV (1920-1), 83-94.

*Duntroon, Argyll (Fort): Christison, D., Anderson, J., and Ross, T., *PSAS* XXXIX (1904-5), 270-85.

*Eilean Buidhe, Kyles of Bute (Fort): Harrison Maxwell, J., *T Glasgow AS* X (1941), 60-70.

*Everly, Caithness (Broch): Anderson, J., *PSAS* XXXV (1900-1), 142-3.

*Foshigarry, N. Uist (Wheel-houses): Beveridge, E., and Callander, J. G., *PSAS* LXV (1930-1), 300-17, 322-57.

*Freswick Links, Canisbay, Caithness (Hut Circle and Souterrain): Edwards, A. J. H., *PSAS* LIX (1924-5), 89-94 and LXI (1926-7), 200-2.

*Freswick Sands, Caithness (Broch): Anderson, J., *PSAS* XXXV (1900-1), 143-4.

*Galson, Lewis (Settlement): Edwards, A. J. H., *PSAS* LVIII (1923-4), 185-202.

*Garry Iochdrach, N. Uist (Wheel-house): Beveridge, E., and Callander, J. G., *PSAS* LXVI (1931-2), 32-42.

*Gripps, Frotoft, Rousay, Orkney (Souterrain): Grant, W. G., *PSAS* LXXIII (1938-9), 273-5.

*Hogsetter (Huxter), Whalsay, Shetland (Blockhouse Fort): Mitchell, A., *PSAS* XV (1880-1), 303-15.

*Hower, Papa Westray, Orkney (Settlement): Traill, W., and Kirkness, W., *PSAS* LXXI (1936-7), 309-22.

*Howmae, N. Ronaldsay, Orkney (Wheel-houses): Traill, W., *PSAS* XIX (1884-5), 23-32 and XXIV (1889-90), 451-61.

*Jarlshof, Shetland (Settlement, Broch and Wheel-houses): Bruce, J., *PSAS* XLI (1906-7), 11-33.

— *: Curle, A. O., *PSAS* LXVIII (1933-4), 224-319.

— *: Hamilton, J. R. C., *Excavations at Jarlshof, Shetland* (London, 1956).

*Keiss, Caithness (Broch): Anderson, J., *PSAS* XXXV (1900-1), 122-7.

*Kildonan Bay, Kintyre, Argyll (Galleried Dun): Fairhurst, H., *PSAS* LXXIII (1938-9), 185-228.

*Kilpheder, S. Uist (Wheel-house): Lethbridge, T. C., *PPS* XVIII (1952), 176-93.

*Kinbrace, Sutherland (Enclosures and Souterrain): Curle, A. O., *PSAS* XLV (1910-11), 18-26.

*Langwell, Caithness (Wag): Curle, A. O., *PSAS* XLVI (1911-12), 77-89.

*Little Dunagoil, Bute (Fort): Marshall, D. N., *T Bute NHS* XVI (1964), 1-69.

*Lochan-an-Gour, Argyll (Fort): Reid, A., *PSAS* XLIII (1908-9), 34-42.

*Luing South Fort, Argyll (Fort): MacNaughton, A., *PSAS* XXV (1890-1), 476-83 and XXVII (1892-3), 375-80.

*Midhouse, Orkney (Souterrain): Craw, J. H., *PSAS* LXV (1930-1), 357-9.

*Midhowe, Rousay, Orkney (Broch): Callander, J. G., and Grant, W. G., *PSAS* LXVIII (1933-4), 444-516.

Mousa, Shetland (Broch): Paterson, J. W., *PSAS* LVI (1921-2), 172-83.

Muckle Skerry, Shetland (Pottery): Longworth, I. G., *PSAS* XCVI (1962-3), 354-5.

*Ness, Caithness (Broch): Anderson, J., *PSAS* XXXV (1900-1), 143.

*Ness of Burgi, Shetland (Blockhouse Fort): Mowbray, C. L., *PSAS* LXX (1935-6), 381-7.

*Nybster, Caithness (Broch): Anderson, J., *PSAS* XXXV (1900-1), 139-42.

*Ousdale, Caithness (Broch): Mackay, J., *PSAS* XXVI (1891-2), 351-7.

*Portnancon, Durness, Sutherland (Souterrain): Buxton, R. J., *PSAS* LXIX (1934-5), 431-3.

*Rahoy, Morvern, Argyll (Dun): Childe, V. G. and Thorneycroft, W., *PSAS* LXXII (1937-8), 23-43.

*Rennibister, Orkney (Souterrain): Marwick, H., *PSAS* LXI (1926-7), 296-301.

Rhufresean, Ardmarnock, Argyll (Fort): Honeyman, J., *T Glasgow AS* (NS) I (1890), 340-2.

*Road, Caithness (Broch): Anderson, J., *PSAS* XXXV (1900-1), 131-9.

*Rudh'an Dunain, Skye (Cave): Scott, W. L., *PSAS* LXVIII (1933-4), 200-23.

*Sae Breck, Esha Ness, Shetland (Broch): Calder, C. S. T., *PSAS* LXXXVI (1951-2), 178-86.

*Skirza Head, Caithness (Broch): Anderson, J., *PSAS* XXXV (1900-1), 144-5.

*Skitten, Caithness (Broch): Calder, C. S. T., *PSAS* LXXXII, (1947-8), 124-45.

*South Unigarth, Sandwick, Orkney (Souterrain): Ritchie, P. R., *PSAS* XCII (1958-9), 118-19.

Sron an Duin, Barra Head, Berneray (Galleried Promontory Fort): Anderson, J., *PSAS* XXVII (1892-3), 281-93.

*Suidhe Chennaidh, Loch Awe, Argyll (Dun): Christison, D., *PSAS* XXV (1890-1), 117-27.

*Tigh na Fiarnain, Durness, Sutherland (Wheel-house): Mathieson, J., *PSAS*
    LIX (1924-5), 221-3.
*Tigh Talamhanta, Allasdale, Barra (Wheel-house): Young, A., *PSAS* LXXXVII
    (1952-3), 80-105.
*Tiree (Souterrains): Goudie, G., *PSAS* LI (1916-17), 100-7.
*Ugadale Point, Kintyre, Argyll (Stack Fort): Fairhurst, H., *PSAS* LXXXVIII
    (1953-5), 15-21.
*Wag of Forse, Latheron, Caithness (Enclosures and Wag): Curle, A. O.,
    PSAS LXXV (1940-1), 23-38, LXXX (1945-6), 11-24, and LXXXII (1947-8),
    275-85.
*Wester Broch, Caithness (Broch): Anderson, J., *PSAS* XXXV (1900-1), 119-22.
*White Gate, Caithness (Broch): Anderson, J., *PSAS* XXXV (1900-1), 127-30.
*Wiltrow, Shetland (Iron Smelting Site): Curle, A. O., *PSAS* LXX (1935-6),
    153-69.

NORTH-EASTERN PROVINCE

General

CHRISTISON, D., 'The Forts, "Camps", and other Field-works of Perth, For-
    far and Kincardine', *PSAS* XXXIV (1899-1900), 43-120.
R.C.A.H.M.(S), *Fife, Kinross and Clackmannan* (1933).
— *The County of Stirling* (1963).
SIMPSON, W. D., *The Province of Mar* (Aberdeen, 1943).
WAINWRIGHT, F. T., *The Souterrains of Southern Pictland* (London, 1962).
WATSON, W. J., 'Circular Forts in Lorn and North Perthshire', *PSAS* XLIX
    (1914-15), 17-32.
— 'The Circular Forts of North Perthshire', *PSAS* XLVII (1912-13), 30-60.
WOODHAM, A. A., 'A Survey of Prehistoric Monuments in the Black Isle',
    PSAS LXXXVIII (1953-5), 65-95.

Individual Sites

*Ardross, Fife (Souterrain): Chalmers, P. M., *PSAS* XL (1905-6), 355-7.
Barmekin of Echt, Aber. (Fort): Simpson, W. D., *PSAS* LIV (1919-20), 45-53.
*Barnhill, Perth (Souterrain): Hutcheson, A., *PSAS* XXXVIII (1903-4), 541-7.
*Borenich, Loch Tummel, Perth (Dun): Watson, W. J., *PSAS* XLIX (1914-15),
    28-32.
*Buchaam, Strathdon, Aber. (Souterrain): Mitchell, A., *PSAS* IV (1861-2),
    436-40.
Burghead, Moray (Fort): Macdonald, J., *PSAS* IV (1860-1), 321-69.
— *: Young, H. W., *PSAS* XXV (1890-1), 435-47.
— *: Young, H. W., *PSAS* XXVII (1892-3), 86-91.

*Carpow, Perth (Native pottery from Roman Fortress): Birley, E., and Dodds, W., *PSAS* xcvi (1962-3), 205-6.

*Castlehill Wood, **Stirl.** (Dun): Feachem, R. W., *PSAS* xc (1956-7), 24-45.

*Castle Law, Abernethy, Perth (Fort): Christison, D., and Anderson, J., *PSAS* xxxiii (1898-9), 13-33.

*Castle Law, Forgandenny, Perth (Fort): Bell, E. W., *PSAS* xxvii (1892-3), 14-22.

*Castle Newe, Aber. (Souterrain, source of armlets): Anon, *PSAS* vi (1864-6), 13-14.

Coldoch, Perth (Broch): Graham, A., *PSAS* lxxxiii (1948-9), 12-14.

*Covesea, Moray (Sculptor's Cave): Benton, S., *PSAS* lxv, (1930-1), 177-216.

*Craigluscar, Fife (Fort): Hogg, A. H. A., *PSAS* lxxxv (1950-1), 165-70.

*Culbin Sands, Moray (Misc): Black, G. F., *PSAS* xxv (1890-1), 484-511.

Deuchny Hill, Kinnoull, Perth (Fort): Boog Watson, J., *PSAS* lvii (1922-3), 303-6.

*Dinnet, Aber. (Circular Enclosures and Souterrain): Abercromby, J., *PSAS* xxxviii (1903-4), 102-22.

Dunnideer, Aber. (Fort): Simpson, W. D., *PSAS* lxix (1934-5), 463-5.

*Dunsinnane, Perth (Fort): Wise, T. A., *PSAS* ii (1855-6), 93-9.

— *: Brown, T., *PSAS* ix (1871-2), 378-80.

*Finavon, Angus (Fort): Childe, V. G., *PSAS* lxix (1934-5), 49-80.

— *: Childe, V. G., *PSAS* lxx (1935-6), 347-52.

*Inchtuthil, Delvine, Perth (Fort): Ross, T., *PSAS* xxxvi (1901-2), 230-4.

*Keir Hill, Gargunnock, Stirl. (Homestead): Maclaren, A., *PSAS* xci (1957-8), 78-83.

*Kempy, Gask, Perth (Fort): Christison, D., *PSAS* xxxv (1900-1), 37-8.

*Loanhead of Daviot, Aber. (Bloomery): Kilbride-Jones, H. E., *PSAS* lxxi (1936-7), 401-5.

*Longforgan, Perth (Souterrain): Wainwright, F. T., *PSAS* lxxxviii (1953-5), 57-64.

*Meikle Reive, Stirl. (Fort): Fairhurst, H., *T Glasgow AS* xiv (1956), 64-89.

*Orchill, Gask, Perth (Fort): Christison, D., *PSAS* xxxv (1900-1), 21-3.

*Pitcur, Angus (Souterrain): MacRitchie, D., *PSAS* xxxiv (1899-1900), 202-14.

*Scotstarvit, Fife (Homestead): Bersu, G., *PSAS* lxxxii (1947-8), 241-63.

Sundayswells, Aber. (find of Iron A pottery): Simpson, W. D., *PSAS* lxxx (1945-6), 148-50.

*Torwood (Tappoch), Stirl. (Broch): Dundas, J., *PSAS* vi (1864-5), 259-65.

— *(outworks): Hunter, D. M., *P Falkirk ANHS* iv (1946-9), 89-107.

*West Grange of Conan, Angus (Souterrain): Jervise, A., *PSAS* iv (1861-2), 492-9.

*West Plean, Stirl. (Homestead): Steer, K. A., *PSAS* lxxxix (1955-6), 227-51.

General

CHRISTISON, D., 'A General View of the Forts, Camps and Motes of Dumfriesshire, with a detailed description of those in Upper Annandale', *PSAS* XXV (1890-1), 198-256.
— : 'Forts, Camps and Motes of the Upper Ward of Lanarkshire', *PSAS* XXIV (1889-90), 281-352.
— : 'The Prehistoric Forts of Ayrshire', *PSAS* XXVII (1892-3), 381-405.
COLES, F. R., 'The Motes, Forts and Doons in the East and West Divisions of the Stewartry of Kirkcudbright', *PSAS* XXVII (1892-3), 92-185.
— : 'The Motes, Forts and Doons of the Stewartry of Kirkcudbright I', *PSAS* XXV (1890-1), 352-96.
— : '— II', *PSAS* XXVI (1891-2), 117-70.
FEACHEM, R. W., 'Iron Age and Mediaeval Monuments in Galloway and Dumfriesshire', *TD & GNHAS* XXXIII (1954-5), 58-65.
NEWALL, F., 'Early Settlement in Renfrewshire', *PSAS* XCV (1961-2), 159-70.
R.C.A.H.M.(S.), *Dumfriesshire* (1920).
— *Stewartry of Kirkcudbright* (1914).
— *Wigtownshire* (1912).
SMITH, J., *Prehistoric Man in Ayrshire* (London, 1895).

Individual Sites

*Aitnock, Dalry, Ayr (Fort): Smith, J., *PSAS* LIII (1918-19), 130-2.
*Birrenswark (Burnswark), Dumfries (Fort): Christison, D., Barbour, J., and Anderson, J., *PSAS* XXXIII (1898-9), 198-249.
*Borness, Kirkcud. (Cave): Corrie, A. J., Clarke, W. B., and Hunt, A. R., *PSAS* X (1872-4), 476-99.
*Cairngryfe, Lanark (Dun): Childe, V. G., *PSAS* LXXV (1940-1), 213-18.
*Carminnow, Kirkcud. (Fort): Childe, V. G., *PSAS* LXX (1935-6), 341-7.
*Castle Haven, Kirkcud. (Galleried Dun): Barbour, J., *PSAS* XLI (1906-7), 68-80.
*Castlehill, Dalry, Ayr (Dun): Smith, J., *PSAS* LIII (1918-19), 123-9.
*Coalhill, Dalry, Ayr (Fort): Smith, J., *PSAS* LIII (1918-19), 132-4.
*Dowalton Loch, Wigtown (Crannog): Stuart, J., *PSAS* VI (1864-5), 114-78.
*Dunbuie, Dunbarton (Dun): Millar, A., *PSAS* XXX (1895-6), 291-308.
*Hyndford, Lanark (Crannog): Munro, R., *PSAS* XXXIII (1898-9), 373-87.
*Lochend, Coatbridge, Lanark (Crannog): Monteith, J., *T Glasgow AS* IX (1937), 26-43.
*Lochlee, Ayr (Crannog): Munro, R., *PSAS* XIII (1878-9), 175-251.
*Milton Loch, Kirkcud. (Crannog): Piggott, C. M., *PSAS* LXXXVII (1952-3), 134-52.
*Mote of Mark, Kirkcud. (Fort): Curle, A. O., *PSAS* XLVIII (1913-14), 125-68.

*Teroy, Wigtown (Broch): Curle, A. O., *PSAS* XLVI (1911-12), 183-8.

*Torrs, Kirkcud. (Cave): Morris, S. V., *PSAS* LXXI (1936-7), 415-30.

*Trusty's Hill, Anwoth, Kirkcud. (Fort): Thomas, A. C., *TD & GNHAS* XXXVIII (1959-60), 58-70.

*Walls Hills, Renfrew (Fort): Newall, F., *Excavations at Walls Hills, Renfrewshire* (Paisley, 1960).

TYNE-FORTH PROVINCE

General

CHRISTISON, D., 'The Forts of Selkirk, the Gala Water, the Southern Slopes of the Lammermoors, and the North of Roxburgh', *PSAS* XXIX (1894-5), 108-79.

— : 'The Prehistoric Forts of Peeblesshire', *PSAS* XXI (1886-7), 13-82.

CRAW, J. H., 'Notes on Berwickshire Forts', *PSAS* LV (1920-1), 231-55.

HOGG, A. H. A., 'Native Settlements of Northumberland', *Ant.* XVII (1943), 136-47.

— : 'A New List of the Native Sites of Northumberland', *PSAN*[4] XI (1946-50), 140-79.

— : 'The Votadini', in Grimes, W. F. (ed.), *Aspects of Archaeology* (London, 1951).

JOBEY, G., 'Some Rectilinear Settlements of the Roman Period in Northumberland', *Arch. Ael.*[4] XXXVIII (1960), 1-38.

— : 'Further Notes on Rectilinear Earthworks in Northumberland: Some Medieval and Later Settlements', *Arch. Ael.*[4] XXXIX (1961), 87-102.

— : 'A Note on Scooped Enclosures in Northumberland', *Arch. Ael.*[4] XL (1962), 47-58.

— : 'Additional Rectilinear Settlements in Northumberland', *Arch. Ael.*[4] XLI (1963), 211-15.

NORTHUMBERLAND COUNTY HISTORY COMMITTEE, *A History of Northumberland*, I-XV (Newcastle, 1893-1939).

R.C.A.H.M.(S), *Berwickshire* (1909 and 1915).

— *East Lothian* (1924).

— *Midlothian and West Lothian* (1929).

— *Peeblesshire* (forthcoming).

— *Roxburghshire* (1956).

— *Selkirkshire* (1957).

Individual Sites

*Archerfield, Dirleton, E. Lothian (Caves): Cree, J. E., *PSAS* XLIII (1908-9), 243-68.

Arthur's Seat and Dunsapie, Queen's Park, Edinburgh (Forts): Stevenson, R. B. K., *PSAS* LXXXI (1946-7), 158-70.

*Blue Crag, Colwell, Northumbd. (Settlement): Ball, T., *PSAN*[4] II (1925-6), 23-4.

*Bonchester Hill, Roxburgh (Fort and Settlement): Curle, A. O., *PSAS* XLIV (1909-10), 225-36.

— *: Piggott, C. M., *PSAS* LXXXIV (1949-50), 113-37.

— (land use): Dimbleby, D. W., *PSAS* XCIII (1959-60), 237-8.

*Bow, Midlothian (Broch): Curle, J., *PSAS* XXVI (1891-2), 68-9.

*Braidwood, Midlothian (Palisaded Settlement and Fort): Stevenson, R. B. K., *PSAS* LXXXIII (1948-9).

— *: Piggott, S., *PSAS* XCI (1957-8), 61-6.

*Bridge House, Wark, Northumbd. (Settlement): Jobey, G., *Arch. Ael.*[4] XXXVIII (1960), 1-32.

*Broomhouse, Edrom, Berwick (Souterrain): Milne Home, D., and Stuart, J., *PSAS* VIII (1868-9), 20-6.

*Carry House, Birtley, Northumbd. (Settlement): Rome Hall, G., *Arch.* XLV (1880), 355-74.

*Castle Law, Glencorse, Midlothian (Fort and Souterrain): Childe, V. G., *PSAS* LXVII (1932-3), 362-88.

— *: Piggott, S. and C. M., *PSAS* LXXXVI (1951-2), 191-4.

*Chester Hill, Hundleshope, Peebles (Fort): Keefe, P. A. M., *PSAS* LXXX (1945-6), 66-72.

The Chesters, Drem, E. Lothian (Fort and Settlement): Cunningham, J. H., *PSAS* XXX (1895-6), 267-9.

*Craig's Quarry, Dirleton, E. Lothian (Fort): Piggott, S. and C. M., *PSAS* LXXXVI (1951-2), 194-6.

— *: Piggott, S., *PSAS* XCI (1957-8), 66-77.

*Crichton, Midlothian (Souterrain): Rosehill, Lord, *PSAS* VIII (1868-9), 105-9.

— (Roman carving): Edwards, A. J. H., *PSAS* LIX (1924-5), 94-5.

*Crock Cleugh, Roxburgh (Homesteads): Steer, K. A., and Keeney, G. S., *PSAS* LXXXI (1946-7), 138-57.

*Earn's Heugh, Coldingham, Berwick (Forts and Settlement): Childe, V. G., and Forde, C. D., *PSAS* LXVI (1931-2), 152-83.

*Edin's Hall, Berwick (Fort, Broch and Settlement): Stuart, J., *PSAS* VIII (1868-9), 41-6.

— *: Turnbull, J., *H Berwick NC* IX (1879-81), 81-99.

*Glenachan Rig, Cardon, Peebles (Palisaded Homestead): Feachem, R. W., *PSAS* XCII (1958-9), 15-24.

*Greaves Ash, Northumbd. (Fort and Settlement): Tate, G., *H Berwick NC* IV (1856-62), 293-316.

*Gubeon Cottage, Morpeth, Northumbd. (Settlement): Jobey, G., *Arch. Ael.*[4] XXXV (1957), 163-79.

*Gullane, E. Lothian (Burials): Ewart, E., and Curle, A. O., *PSAS* XLII (1907-8), 332-41.

*Gunnar Peak, Chollerton, Northumbd. (Settlement): Rome Hall, G., *Arch. Ael.*² X (1884), 12-37.

*Harehope, Peebles (Palisaded Settlement): Feachem, R. W., *PSAS* XCIII (1959-60), 174-91.

*Hayhope Knowe, Morebattle, Roxburgh (Palisaded Settlement): Piggott, C. M., *PSAS* LXXXIII (1948-9), 45-67.

*Hownam Rings, Morebattle, Roxburgh (Palisaded Settlement, Fort and Settlement): Piggott, C. M., *PSAS* LXXXII (1947-8), 193-224.

*Huckhoe, Northumbd. (Palisaded and Walled Settlement): Jobey, G., *Arch. Ael.*⁴ XXXVII (1959), 217-78.

*Ingram Hill, Northumbd. (Palisaded and Walled Settlement): Hogg, A. H. A., *Arch. Ael.*⁴ XX (1942), 110-33.

— *: Hogg, A. H. A., *Arch. Ael.*⁴ XXXIV (1956), 150-60.

Kaimes Hill, Midlothian (Fort and Settlement): Coles, F. R., *PSAS* XXX (1895-6), 269-74.

— *: Childe, V. G., *PSAS* LXXV (1940-1), 43-54.

Manor, Peebles (Scooped Enclosures): Stevenson, R. B. K., *PSAS* LXXV (1940-1), 92-115.

*Marden, Tynemouth, Northumbd. (Settlement): Jobey, G., *Arch. Ael.*⁴ XLI (1963), 19-36.

*Milking Gap, High Shield, Northumbd. (Settlement): Kilbride-Jones, H. E., *Arch. Ael.*⁴ XV (1938), 303-50.

*Moredun, Gilmerton, Midlothian (Cist Burial): Coles, F. R., *PSAS* XXXVIII (1903-4), 427-38.

*Old Bewick, Northumbd. (Settlement): Charlton, J., *PSAN*⁴ VI (1933-4), 252-6.

*Riding Wood, Bellingham, Northumbd. (Settlement): Jobey, G., *Arch. Ael.*⁴ XXXVIII (1960), 1-32.

Ruberslaw, Roxburgh (Fort): Curle, A. O., *PSAS* XXXIX (1904-5), 219-32.

— *: Curle, A. O., *PSAS* XLI (1906-7), 451-3.

Smalesmouth, Northumbd. (Settlement): Jobey, G., *Arch. Ael.*⁴ XXXIX (1961), 371-3.

*Stanhope, Peebles (Dun): Maclaren, A., *PSAS* XCIII (1959-60), 192-201.

*Throckington Quarry House, Northumbd. (Settlement): Hedley, R. C., *Arch. Ael.*² XII (1886), 155-8.

Torwoodlee, Selkirk (Fort and Broch): Curle, J., *PSAS* XXVI (1891-2), 71-84.

— *: Piggott, S., *PSAS* LXXXV (1950-1), 92-117.

*Traprain Law, E. Lothian (Fort): Curle, A. O., *PSAS* XLIX (1914-15), 139-202.

— *: Curle, A. O. and Cree, J. E., *PSAS* L (1915-16), 64-144.

— *: Curle, A. O., *PSAS* LIV (1919-20), 54-123.

— *: Curle, A. O., and Cree, J. E., *PSAS* LV (1920-1), 153-206.

— *: Cree, J. E., and Curle, A. O., *PSAS* LVI (1921-2), 189-260.

— *: Cree, J. E., *PSAS* LVII (1922-3), 180-225.

— *: Cree, J. E., *PSAS* LVIII (1923-4), 241-85.

— *: Cruden, S. H., *PSAS* LXXIV (1939-40), 48-59.

— *: Bersu, G., *Scot. Reg. Group*, C.B.A., *Second Report* (1948), 5.

— : Feachem, R. W., *PSAS* LXXXIX (1955-6), 284-9.

*West Longlee, Wark, Northumbd. (Settlement): Jobey, G., *Arch. Ael.*[4] XXXVIII (1960), 1-32.

*Witchy Neuk, Hepple, Northumbd. (Settlement): Wake, T., *Arch. Ael.*[4] XVI (1939), 129-39.

*Yevering Bell, Northumbd. (Fort): Tate, G., *H Berwick NC* IV (1856-62), 431-53.

PENNINE AND EASTERN PROVINCES

General

BLAKE, B., 'Excavations on Native (Iron Age) Sites in Cumberland 1956-58 (Old Brampton, Jacob's Gill (Rosley), Wolsty Hall and Risehow (Maryport))', *TC & WAAS* LIX (1960), 1-14.

ELGEE, F., *Early Man in North-East Yorkshire* (Gloucester, 1930).

ELGEE, F. and H. W., *The Archaeology of Yorkshire* (London, 1933).

FERGUSON, R. S. and SWAINSON COWPER, H., 'An Archaeological Survey of Cumberland and Westmorland and of Lancashire North-of-the-Sands', *Arch.* LIII (1893), 485-538.

R.C.H.M.(E), *Westmorland* (1936).

STEAD, I. M., *La Tène Cultures of East Yorkshire* (York, 1965).

Victoria County History of Durham I (London, 1905).

Individual Sites

*Ewe Close, Westmorland (Settlement): Collingwood, W. G., *TC & WAAS* VIII (1908), 355-68 and IX (1909), 295-309.

Lune Valley (Celtic Fields and Homesteads): Lowndes, R. A. C., *TC & WAAS* LXIII (1963), 77-95.

*Skelmore Heads, Ulverston, Lancs (Fort): Powell, T. G. E., *TC & WAAS* LXIII (1963), 1-30.

*Stanwick, N.R. Yorks (Fort): Wheeler, R. E. M., *The Stanwick Fortifications*, Soc. of Ants. Research Report XVII (London, 1954).

*Staple Howe, E.R. Yorks (Settlement): Brewster, T. C. M., *The Excavation of Staple Howe* (Scarborough, 1963).

*West Brandon, Durham (Homestead): Jobey, G., *Arch. Ael.*[4] XL (1962), 1-34.

GEOGRAPHICAL INDEX

The following abbreviations have been used to indicate page references to a diagram: (d), map: (m), plan: (p), table: (t) and folding map: (fm). An asterisk indicates the page, or facing page, reference for an illustration.

GENERAL INDEX

'Abernethy' complex, 10, 20, 21, 66
Agricola, Cn. Julius, 52
aisled houses, *see under* wheel-houses
Alcock, L., 33
Allen, D.F., 22, 25
Anderson, Joseph, 1, 111
Anglo-Saxons, 37
armlets, bronze, 10, 12, 31, 32, 32*, 34(m)
axes, iron, 18(m), 20

Bede, 52
belt-plate, enamelled, 32
'birrens', 76, 101
bits, *see under* horse-gear
blockhouses, 113(p), 116, 117*, 120, 120*,
    121-5
bobbins, bone, 11
bone, objects of, *see* bobbins, darts, dice,
    loop-handle, toggles, weaving combs
boss style, 31-2
bowls, bronze, 12, 31
bracelets, snake, 32, 32*, 34(m)
brochs, 9, 11, 32, 33(m), 35, 44-58, 85-6,
    111, 112*, 113*, 113(p), 114(d), 115-28,
    120*, (fm); *see also* duns
Bronze Age, in Scotland, 2-3, 6-7, 19, 48, 77
bronze, objects of, *see* metal-work, armlets,
    belt-plate, bowls, brooches, carnyx,
    cauldrons, collars, dress-fasteners,
    horse-gear, mirrors, pins, razors, rings,
    sheet bronze, spoons, swords, scabbards
    and chapes, tankard handle, torcs
brooches
    Aucissa type (similar to), 25
    Colchester type, 25
    dragonesque, 19*, 29(m), 30-1
    head-stud, 31
    Langton Down type, 25
    la Tène 1c, 8, 9, 10, 18(m), 19*, 20
    la Tène I-II, 20
    la Tène II derivative, 25
    la Tène III, 22
    penannular, 9, 19*, 25
    Polden Hill type, 25
    zoomorphic, 37
burials, 25
Burning of Da Derga's Hostel, 121-5

Caesar, C. Julius, 7, 127
Calder, C.S.T., 115

carnyx, bronze, 12, 24, 31*, 32
carved stone balls (neolithic or bronze age),
    36(m), 37
cauldrons, bronze, 12, 31
Celts, social customs of, 120-7
'chamfrein', *see* pony-cap *under* horse-gear
chapes, *see under* swords
cheekpiece, *see under* horse-gear
Childe, V.G., 1, 17, 19, 20, 26, 28, 37, 66, 112
Christison, D., 1
cisterns, rock-hewn, in forts, 68
coins, Celtic, 22, 24
Coles, J.M., 3, 7, 17, 19
collar, hinged, 10, 11, 32, 33*
Cotton, Mrs M.A., 7, 21, 66, 67, 118
crannogs, 9, 11, 21, 25, 26, 28, 33(m)
cultivation terraces, 105
Curle, James, 1, 31, 35

darts, bone, 127
dating of phases of the Iron Age, 3-13
Davidson, J.L., 65
Diarmuid and Grainne, 122
dice, bone, 11
dress-fasteners, 30. 31, 32
duns, 10, 47, 85-6, 114-15, 119(p), (fm);
    see also brochs, forts

earth-houses, *see* souterrains
enamelwork, 32, 37
enclosures, *see* scooped enclosures, settle-
    ments

farms, *see* homesteads, settlements
Feachem, R.W., 3, 31, 37, 59-87
fibulae, *see* brooches
fire, use of, in attacking forts, 127
forts, iron-age
    general, 7-10, 19, 20, 25, 28, 30, 59-86,
        95-100
    'birrens', 76, 101
    cisterns in, 68
    'citadel forts', 82-5
    distribution of, 85-6, 64(m), 78(m),
        90(m), (fm)
    multivallation, 10, 69-70
    murus duplex, 114(d)
    oppida, 77-85, 78(m)
    overlaid by settlements, 90(m), 97, 101-4,

153

LEARNING RESOURCES

CENTER

East Peoria, Illinois